The Fertile Soil of Jihad

RELATED TITLES FROM POTOMAC BOOKS

Jihad Joe: Americans Who Go to War in the Name of Islam
—J. M. Berger

Radical Islam in America: Salafism's Journey from Arabia to the West
—Chris Heffelfinger

"My Heart Became Attached": The Strange Journey of John Walker Lindh
—Mark Kukis

Virtual Caliphate: Exposing the Islamist State on the Internet
—Yaakov Lappin

The Path to Paradise: The Inner World of Suicide Bombers and Their Dispatchers
—Anat Berko

The Banality of Suicide Terrorism: The Naked Truth About the Psychology of Islamic Suicide Bombing
—Nancy Hartevelt Kobrin

The Fertile Soil of Jihad

Terrorism's Prison Connection

PATRICK T. DUNLEAVY

Potomac Books
An imprint of the University of Nebraska Press

Library of Congress Cataloging-in-Publication Data

Dunleavy, Patrick T.
The fertile soil of jihad : terrorism's prison connection / Patrick T. Dunleavy.—1st ed.
p. cm.
Includes bibliographical references and index.
ISBN 978-1-59797-548-3 (hardcover: alk. paper)
ISBN 978-1-61234-114-9 (electronic edition)
1. Terrorists—Recruiting—United States. 2. Prisoners—United States—Social conditions. 3. Prisoners—Religious life—United States. 4. Muslim prisoners—United States. 5. Terrorism—Religious aspects—Islam. I. Title.
HV6432.D86 2011
363.325'11—dc22

2011013961

Printed in the United States of America on acid-free paper that meets the American National Standards Institute Z39-48 Standard.

First Edition

To the memory of my parents:
Charles Francis Dunleavy, a distinguished veteran
and a member of the Greatest Generation;
and Noreen Bernadette Fahy, who taught me
that reading books is one of the greatest
pleasures in life.

And to all those who have gone before us
in the fight against terrorism.

Midway in our life's journey, I went astray
from the straight road and woke to find myself
alone in a dark wood. How shall I say

what wood that was! I never saw so drear, so
rank, so arduous a wilderness!
Its very memory gives a shape to fear.

Death could scarce be more bitter than that place! . . .

so did I turn, my soul still fugitive
from death's surviving image, to stare down
that pass that none had ever left alive. . . .

I entered on that hard and perilous track. . . .

ABANDON ALL HOPE YE WHO ENTER HERE.

These mysteries I read cut into stone
above a gate. . . .

. . . "Woe to you depraved souls!
Bury here and forever all hope of Paradise:
I come to lead you to the other shore, into eternal dark."

—*The Inferno* by Dante Alighieri,
translated by John Ciardi (1954)

Contents

Acknowledgments

This book could not have been written without the help and encouragement of my friends and colleagues. John Cutter, former deputy chief of NYPD Intelligence, provided the historical insight on the formation of the Regional Intelligence and Fusion Centers now being used across the nation. John Bilich, former deputy commissioner of Criminal Justice Services, taught me never to exhaust a lead—to run the race until the end and to keep your chest out as you cross the finish line. Kenneth Torreggiani, deputy inspector general and member of the FBI's Joint Terrorist Task Force (JTTF), provided insight into the world of confidential informants, having worked in that field for more than twenty-five years. Vern Fonda, Chief of Investigations for the Department of Correctional Services, has served the people of New York for more than thirty years, diffusing volatile situations with tactical experience second to none.

Thank you to my friend and mentor, the late Brian Francis Malone, special prosecutor for the Attica Commission and New York Inspector General from 1975 to 2001.

Sincere gratitude to Frank Straub, former Naval Intelligence and NYPD Deputy Commissioner, for his guidance and wisdom.

Thanks to those who worked in Operation Hades, from the green-eyed cultural analysts to the seasoned detectives of the NYPD: James Murphy, David Miller, Danny Coats, Ira Greenberg, Milton Lopez, Jimmy Maxson, Rolando Rivera, Curtis Culbreth, Sonny Serrano, Billy Blendermann, and the late Matty Rosenthal; the individuals from the CIA (who shall remain anonymous) I met one night in a warehouse in Queens; James Maxwell from the JTTF New York office; those from Scotland Yard, Shin Bet, and the Canadian Intelligence Services who provided assistance; and Chris Renny from the Toronto Police Department. There are those yet unnamed who still fight the hardest in this battle.

Madeleine Gruen, counterterrorism senior analyst, was an invaluable source of guidance and direction. She was the sensei and I a mere grasshopper.

The writing of this book was often an arduous affair that would not have been completed without the belief of others who at times had more faith than I did. To APR, who always believed that this book was going to happen, you were an inspiring influence of encouragement. Thank you. I also have to acknowledge my sons, Andrew, Mark, and Timothy, who when they were young often had no idea what their father did and now as men have become my greatest advisers.

I've often read acknowledgments in other books in which the authors thanked their agents and pondered what I would write about mine. Kelly Fisher, aka "Irish," was to me a second voice who often knew what I wanted to say before I said it. It is not easy for a cop to write about police work for those who have not been in the arena. We are insular, have our own language and idioms, and often stumble over our words with civilians. I spent long periods of time during the editing process explaining to Irish how intelligence, police work, and covert surveillance operated, only to hear her say again and again, "Well, why don't you just write it like that?" Without her I would never have found my voice.

Much thanks to Hilary Claggett of Potomac Books for her gracious thoughts, words of encouragement, and her devotion of time and energy to seeing the proposal become a manuscript and the manuscript become a book.

My sincere appreciation to my editor, Don McKeon, for his strict adherence to detail, his patience, and his guidance in getting me through the process and teaching me the best way to translate a thought into written form.

And finally, to my wife, Linda, for her love and support. Thirty-six years ago she met a young man who was described to her as an aspiring writer. Life took a longer path, but after all those years, Linda, you finally got a book from me.

Preface

On January 26, 1993, a young Palestinian immigrant was arrested in New York City for a series of kidnappings and robberies. Thirty days later, while he was being held in the city's prison complex at Rikers Island, awaiting trial in Manhattan, a rental truck with fifteen hundred pounds of explosives was detonated in the garage of the World Trade Center by Islamic terrorists. This first attack on American soil ushered in the beginning of the jihad and with it the war on terrorism.

A few years later, things really began to heat up. In 1998, two U.S. embassies in Africa were bombed. December 1999 brought the arrest of Ahmed Ressam, an al Qaeda operative caught by U.S. Border Patrol in Washington State for attempting to smuggle nitroglycerin in his car. Ressam was part of an intricate plot to blow up Los Angeles International Airport on New Year's Eve. It would have been the jihadists' second act on American soil.

As early as February 1999, the FBI had received information from two independent sources that Middle Eastern inmates within the American prison system were undertaking a recruitment effort to produce a crop of homegrown terrorists. These leads, like seed, fell along the wayside and were not taken seriously.

In the immediate aftermath of 9/11, these same law enforcement and intelligence agencies scrambled to find any other imminent threats, including "sleeper cells" operating on American soil. The old leads were examined and reexamined, and from that a name surfaced—Abdel Nasser Zaben, that same Palestinian arrested in 1993.

This seemingly common criminal was turning out to be not common at all. He had sworn his allegiance to Osama bin Laden and had been converting fertile young minds in the soil of prison to the terrorist cause.

Following 9/11, Glenn Goord, the commissioner of New York State's Department of Correctional Services (NYDOCS), appointed me deputy inspector general of the department's Criminal Intelligence Unit. I became part of Operation Hades, an investigation conducted by federal, state, and city law enforcement and intelligence agencies that probed the radical Islamic recruitment movement for jihad from both inside and outside prison walls. This book, in part, is inspired by that investigation and the men and women who worked the cases. It answers an important two-fold question: How is it possible to grow a terrorist cell, and can this be done within a prison?

The Fertile Soil of Jihad is about terrorism recruitment inside prison—where it starts, how it develops, and the belief that where one cell ends, another begins. Jihad isn't a singular idea that stops when discovered; jihad is a cultural and religious war that has no end. Likewise, the people involved in jihad don't stop their efforts when incarcerated. They just find another path—new and clever ways to achieve their goal.

A terrorist is not hatched overnight. A person, radical or not, is a sum of many parts, made up of cultural background, influences, and experiences. This book details the progression of a prisoner from common crook to jihadist, examining in particular detail what happened to Zaben, whose background shaped the terrorist he became and the actions he took.

After the first World Trade Center attack, authorities believed that the terrorist cell responsible for that act, created by El Sayyid Nosair, had been dismembered. After following leads that directed them to Zaben and the recruitment work he had been doing in prison, they were forced to reconsider. Based on data analysis, including statements from confidential sources, recorded conversations, common addresses, and mosque affiliations, they knew that Zaben was connected to Nosair, Abdel Rahman (also known as the Blind Sheikh), and others convicted in the 1993 World Trade Center bombing. This book reveals how Zaben's efforts were discovered and how authorities were able to monitor, infiltrate, and neutralize the cell before it could act.

Zaben's story is a fascinating case study in how the prison subculture fosters terrorism. Knowing the typical profiles of potential terrorists long before the CIA and FBI outlined their findings in 2003, Zaben carefully selected the most likely candidates for conversion to his terrorist cause. He was born and raised in the soil of conflict, and he found purpose in the prison of his enemies, sowing the seeds of jihad among others like him who were disenfranchised and angry. He learned how to utilize the prison resources available to him—the phone system, visitor privileges, and the commissary account, for example—for terrorist motives. He also learned how to use his apprentice role in the prison chaplain's office as a cover and command center for his work.

In the period between the first and second World Trade Center attacks, many believe that the government and the public became complacent. Since 9/11 much has been done to keep us both aware and vigilant. We will forever need such vigilance, for the Zabens of this world are always looking for an opening.

CHAPTER 1

The Haj Westward

The command is issued, "On the count." In the background prisoners shout the jailhouse jargon, "Yo, yo, C.O.—hold up!" But the corrections officer doesn't stop and in fact methodically marches from one end of the gallery to the other. Looking, he counts living, breathing bodies of flesh. That's all that matters.

As the cellblock captain walks, the repetitive *clank clank clank* echoes—the sound of steel doors slamming against concrete walls. Inside, another inmate lies alone in this abyss the prisoners call Hades. Reduced to a number, Abdel Nasser Zaben lies on his bunk dreaming of another time in another world when he was close to his family. He hears again the words of his father, "*A salam alaikum, enshallah* [Peace be upon you, if it is God's will], my son; remember your duty to prayer and may God keep you while you are among the unbelievers. You are *ibn Islam*"—a son of Islam. With these words, the old man had kissed his son goodbye. But he was not just another father sending his son away from war, on a journey to seek peace and prosperity in a far-off land.

In Islam there are five duties—Pillars of Islam—incumbent on every true believer. The first is *shahada*: the declaration of faith. The second is *sala*: prayer, required five times a day. The third is *zakat*: giving alms for charity and for personal redemption. The fourth is *saum*: fasting during Ramadan. The fifth is *haj*: the journey. Normally when a young Muslim man goes on a *haj*, he heads to Mecca in Saudi Arabia. Zaben, however, was not going that way. Instead, he was heading west, to America.

Zaben's journey to America started from Ramallah in the Israeli-occupied West Bank. He had been born in a refugee camp on the East Bank of the Jordan River in 1969, where his parents, along with thousands of Palestinians, had relocated after the formation of the nation of Israel in 1948.[1]

Among those who had moved were Abdallah Azzam and Ali Kased, contemporaries of Zaben's father. Both men left the camps to study in Cairo and went on to become key figures in Islam and the Palestinian struggle. While in Egypt, they became well acquainted with the Muslim Brotherhood and its jihadist networks in the Middle East. Radical Islam's influence on Zaben had started at an early age.

After teaching in the refugee camps, Azzam went on to be credited as the original architect of global jihad. In 1981, he went to Saudi Arabia to teach at the University at Jeddah. He engrained in his students that the struggle for Islam was not to be confined to national borders or the occupied territories; the battle went beyond nationalism. One of his students was a young engineering major named Osama bin Laden.

Kased was born in the West Bank town of Ein Yabrud, just six years before the nation of Israel was formed and the diaspora of almost one million Palestinians, including Kased's family. As a teenager he became involved in the movement for the return of the Palestinians to what they considered occupied territory. He fled to Egypt and enrolled at American University, majoring in economics and political science. Following his studies in Cairo and the defeat of Egypt in the 1967 war with Israel, Kased went through a defining transformation. He became an avowed militant in the fight to destroy Israel. He became one of the founders of the Popular Front for the Liberation of Palestine (PFLP). A short time later in 1969, he immigrated to the United States and opened a coffee shop on Atlantic Avenue in Brooklyn. He devoted his spare time to raising money for the Palestinian cause and educating both students and others about the struggle.[2] Kased maintained ties with friends and families on the West Bank and often provided a place to stay or a job for the sons and daughters of old neighbors. Many of those who were making their journey to the United States found the trip difficult physically, financially, and emotionally.

Movement for Palestinians was tightly controlled and fraught with perils for anyone but especially for Zaben, the nephew of Khalil al-Zaben, a high-ranking member of Yasser Arafat's inner circle.[3] His immediate and extended family was from Ramallah as well, where the headquarters of Palestinian Liberation Organization (PLO) was located, along with the residence of PLO leader Yasser Arafat.

In the occupied territories at the time, the PLO was one of more than a dozen groups representing the Palestinian people's cause. Other groups included the PFLP, the Abu Nidal Organization, Al-Fatah, Islamic Jihad, Hezbollah, and Hamas. Zaben had chosen to be a member of Hamas owing to its Sunni Muslim religious fervor and doctrine. He had attended various mosques in the occupied territories and had listened to speeches of radical Islamic clerics such as Sheikh Ahmed Yassin and Abu Hassan Musaab. Yassin was one of Hamas's founders and its spiritual leader. Hamas grew out of the Muslim Brotherhood movement, founded in 1928 by Hasan al Banna in Egypt. From there it moved into various Islamic countries, including Palestine. In December 1986 seven Palestinian members of the Brotherhood met secretly in the city of Hebron on the West Bank, with the goal of creating an organization that would take direct action against the Israelis.[4] They began looking for an incident by Israel, however small, that would be an impetus to violent jihad in both Gaza and the West Bank.

Zaben was also familiar with Marwan Al-Barghouti, a noted Al-Fatah leader, but felt that out of all the groups, only Hamas and Islamic Jihad were united in supporting their leaders against the Israelis. Despite their unification for the same cause, Zaben spoke out angrily against Al-Fatah, saying, "The Fatah guys, when they [Israelis] arrested their guy no one [in Al-Fatah] said anything. They were . . . like mice."[5]

Zaben saw the Israelis as an inferior enemy occupying force, calling them "cowards" and "pigs." Zaben did not and could not separate his hatred for his enemies and his fervency for his religion: both were equally strong. In Zaben's mind these two feelings—hatred for Jews and love for Allah—were inseparable. He made this clear in a conversation with one of his sisters: "Whatever Allah wants to happen to you is going to happen, it is too late . . . they [Israelis] are doing that to you so you surrender to them." His sister replied, "*Enshallah*, we will never do that." Zaben went on to say, "They [Israelis] are living in fear more than we are . . . they sit in the bus, they don't know who is a Jew and who is the one who is going to blow himself up. . . . They [Jews] are cowards and may Allah break them down . . . may Allah set you free from them."[6]

With regard to Islam he once told a friend, "By Allah . . . Islam and Muslims, as we know, are the strongest when they are under hard attack, as what happened with Abu Bakr. . . . They [Muslims] show their best power." (Abdel was referring to Prophet Muhammad's father-in-law and the first Muslim caliph, who laid the foundation for an Islamic empire in the seventh century.) Abdel went on to say, "As Sheikh [Yusef] Al-Qaradawi has said . . . we will never get dignity without Islam, never, we just want Allah to unify the Muslims and give them their dignity back."[7]

On December 9, 1987, when Zaben was about eighteen years old, four refugees in Gaza were killed in an accident involving an Israeli vehicle. In the Jabalia refugee camp, Palestinians began to protest. During the protest, one refugee was shot and killed by Israeli soldiers. This was the fuse that set off the powder keg known as the First Intifada (*intifada* is an Arabic word that means a shaking off, sudden waking from sleep, or uprising). Protests spread immediately from Gaza to Nablus, to Ramallah and East Jerusalem,[8] resulting in work stoppage, school and store closings, boycotts, and civil disobedience in the street on a daily basis. Demonstrations then progressed to groups of Palestinian teenagers throwing rocks at Israeli tanks and armored vehicles, causing violent confrontations with the Israel Defense Forces.

Experts disagree as to the duration of the First Intifada. Some believe it subsided in 1991 after the Madrid Conference on Middle East Conflict, whereas others cite the end as the Oslo Accords of 1993. The First Intifada's significance was in establishing the credentials of Hamas. Because the leadership of the PLO was still in exile in Cyprus at the time, a large majority of Palestinians viewed the new Hamas organization as not only speaking for them but also being involved on the ground—not ruling from afar. This did much to capture their hearts and create animosity toward the PLO and its offshoot, Al-Fatah. This animosity would later drive a violent wedge between the people, pitting Palestinian against Palestinian.

Being a young man at this time on the West Bank was anything but a guarantee for a long and prosperous life. Each person had to choose a side in the complicated battle, and Zaben believed that in order to have fulfillment, he must take up the Palestinian struggle, which he believed was also Allah's cause. He demonstrated this some years later in a conversation with an American Muslim who had returned from an Islamic religious school, or *madrassa*, in Egypt, when he said,

> By Allah, we have a saying, "If you are no good to your own people, how can you be good to others?" Do you understand me? It is impossible, impossible. . . . Some Muslims want to stay in the middle, I mean, not with us and not with them...but the Government is going to make them decide whether you are with them or with us. You remember what the President [George W. Bush] said, "You're with us or you're with them." He is going to make the Muslims say, "We are with Islam!" *Enshallah*. He is going to make them say that. By Allah we will never have dignity without Islam—never, no, by God, no.

Being neutral was dangerous, and Zaben went on in the conversation to warn against the danger of betraying your own people: "If he puts a *kaffeya* [Palestinian headwear] on and acts nonsense . . . they know who is good and who is not . . . and boom they end up dead!"[9]

From 1987 through 1991 it was estimated that more than one thousand Palestinians were killed by Israeli forces. The various factions representing the Palestinian people also had violent differences and infighting among themselves. An estimated two hundred to one thousand Palestinians suspected of cooperating with the Israelis were killed by their fellow Arabs. They were bludgeoned by axes, shot, clubbed, and burned with acid—in executions carried out by death squads or hired killers approved by the PLO.[10]

Yes, a side had to be chosen. And from their sleep, the Palestinians on the West Bank and Gaza woke up with a vengeance—throwing rocks, Molotov cocktails, grenades, and bombs at the Israeli occupying forces. Saying that it was simply a troubled time minimizes the violence and hatred that was the breeding ground for young Zaben. "Jihad" had real meaning to a Muslim family like his living on the West Bank in 1990. They had been hearing about it since they were in the refugee camps from men like Abdallah Azzam and Ali Kased. Families willingly gave up their young to become suicide bombers (*mujahideen*), considered holy warriors in the struggle. Along with Zaben's family, at least three other Palestinian families from both the West Bank and Gaza sent their sons abroad: the Al-Zahaars, Abu-Shanabs, and the Al-Rantisis.[11] Abdul Aziz Al-Rantisi, a future leader of Hamas, sent one of his sons to Iraq. His other sons were encouraged to be suicide bombers.

Zaben was about twenty years old at the time he was sent on his journey. He had two brothers and two sisters and loved his family, especially his mother. His oldest brother, Yousef, was already in the

United States, living in a luxury apartment on Shore Road in Brooklyn overlooking New York Harbor. His younger brother, Sayeed, and his two sisters remained in Ramallah along with Amin and Ayman, his nephews. Ayman Zaben later came to worldwide attention in 2007 when he was identified as a member of a terrorist group captured on the West Bank by the Israelis. He had been a fugitive since October 2000, when he and sixteen other members of Tanzim Fatah beat and lynched two Israeli soldiers at a Palestinian police station in Ramallah. Graphic video of the officers being hanged and then thrown out of a window to an angry mob and the mutilation of their bodies was flashed around the world.[12]

When Abdel Nasser Zaben left, he took with him photos of his family, which became his most cherished possessions. He embarked on his pilgrimage to New York not knowing if he would ever see his mother alive again. Years later, much different photos than those of his family would surface showing him wearing military fatigues and brandishing automatic weapons. He would use those photos as recruitment posters.[13]

As a good Muslim, Zaben had memorized portions of the Koran. Before he left, he had also memorized the names and addresses of contacts and important places, such as his post office box in Panama where monies were received from the United States and forwarded to the Middle East. If someone was anticipating travel between New York and the Middle East (especially for nefarious reasons), it was important that the route of the sent items be untraceable. Panama was the perfect place to send money or route people. Ships were not the only thing that passed through the Canal.

In his first attempt to enter New York City in the spring of 1990, when he was twenty years old, Zaben made it only as far as JFK International Airport. Attempting to gain entry with a forged student visa, he was quickly taken into custody by personnel of the Immigration and Naturalization Service (INS). He was then held in a detention center on the airport grounds operated by Wackenhut Industries, a private company under contract with the federal government.[14]

Prior to the World Trade Center bombing, no watch list was in existence for young Muslim men being held in a private prison. Companies were awarded contracts with the government to operate correctional facilities in an attempt to save the government the cost of building and staffing the additional space needed for an increased number of prisoners. Corporations such as Wackenhut operated from a supply-side economic philosophy. What mattered was the number of people being held in their detention centers, not *who*. Numbers meant money.

A young man with a forged visa was not that uncommon and rarely seen as the potential beginning of a "cell," that smallest of organisms representing the vanguard of a terrorist organization on foreign soil. The U.S. government should have been more careful, but it was largely unaware at that time of the resentment felt by many Muslims. They were upset about the abandonment of the *mujahideen* in Afghanistan by the United States and their perception that America was favoring Israel in the fight for "the Land." It was a resentment that bred anger, which would then incite action.

During his detention, Zaben was routinely questioned and processed. There were no unusual notations in his INS folder, only the word "overstayed" stamped inside that made it sound like he was merely someone who checked out late from a hotel. Less than two weeks after this first apprehension, Zaben was deported back to Jordan.

In hindsight, more than ten years later, the oversight by INS was significant enough to cause concern when a request was made by members of Operation Hades to review the entries in Zaben's immigration folder.[15] Had they failed to take proper action? Once again, they should have paid more attention to detail. Some INS documents on Zaben's entries into the United States are unclear and conflict with statements he made to confidential sources with regard to his movement prior to his arrival. In those conversations, Zaben said that his journey had taken him through the free trade zone in Panama. According to documentation, Zaben lived only in New York, but he also spoke with surprising familiarity about Texas, Louisiana, Pennsylvania, and other places in the United States. Authorities believed that he had established contacts prior to his imprisonment. In 2004 documentation confirmed his contacts in Texas when his brother Sayeed planned to visit him there from the West Bank.

In a small Texas town called Mesquite, approximately fifteen miles southeast of the Dallas suburb of Richardson, investigators from Operation Hades were monitoring phone calls from the Middle East when they learned of plans for Sayeed Zaben to come to the United States. Initially investigators believed he would simply visit his brother in New York. However, tracking Sayeed's every movement from the time his plane landed, members of Operation Hades watched him travel to Pennsylvania, North Carolina, Louisiana, and ultimately Texas to take up residence. Sayeed then used the address 2023 Hillcrest Street, apt. 2083, Mesquite, Texas, to obtain a driver's license only thirty days after he arrived from the Middle East.[16] He did this after 9/11, when safeguards were supposedly in place by the newly created Department of Homeland Security to prevent foreigners from gaining a driver's license without proper background checks for residency and identification—a process that would take much longer than thirty days.

This made it clear to investigators that there was a long-standing network, going all the way back to Zaben's initial arrival in 1990, to help newly arrived Muslims, jihadists even, obtain documents and move throughout the United States unimpeded. Much of the support came from Saudi Arabia through the Islamic Center in Richardson, which was associated with a mosque.[17] According to sources, Zaben attended Jummah services there,[18] finding fellow believers who helped him on his way. They were good brothers at the center, and they helped to raise money for the plight of the Palestinians as well as other Islamic charities. After all, *zakat* (almsgiving) is the third tenet of Islam, commanded by Muhammad. Little was known at the time by the U.S. Internal Revenue Service or other federal agencies charged with oversight where these monies wound up. Charities such as Help the Needy, the Al-Kifah Refugee Fund, the Holy Land Foundation, and others were merely a way for Muslims in America to fulfill one of their obligations of faith. We now know, however, that some of the monies raised by these charities went directly to finance terrorist organizations.[19]

Back in New York, Ali Kased had raised significant amounts for Al-Awda/Palestinian Right to Return Coalition and the Palestinian Children's Relief Fund (PCRF),[20] among other charities. Without these funds, organizations such as PFLP and Hamas could not operate. Every jihadist knew this, but most Muslims would not give their alms willingly to finance guns and bombs. As a result, the jihadists found it necessary to create charities that gave the appearance of good works—helping to build schools and medical facilities—while discreetly siphoning some of the funds for fighters. Money was always important to the movement, and obscuring the source and the destination was vital to assuring that the sending of that money would not be interrupted.[21]

In the beginning of his journey, Zaben was encouraged to continue in the faith and attend Jummah services regularly in whatever city he found himself. He was provided with the names of several *masjids* where good Muslim brothers practiced Sharia law and attended the mosques for *Hayya'ala's Sala*, or call to prayer. His hope was that regular attendance would keep him from backsliding into the ways of the world.

Two *masjids* recommended to him were Al Farooq and Al Taqwa.[22] Since both were located in New York City, Zaben packed up, left Texas, and headed north. He arrived in New York with his luggage and a visitor's visa in hand, just another tourist stopping to stare at the tall buildings and the lights of the skyline. All he needed was a copy of *Fodor's Travel Guide* under his arm, and he would have fit right in. Looks, however, can be deceiving. Zaben was not simply another traveler intending to take in the attractions. He was a soldier of jihad.

Zaben had seen his first attempt to enter New York City as an embarrassment, yes, but it was only a mere bump on the road to his ultimate goal. He had not obtained a good view of the West then—he was in Texas less than a month—but he was about to. Attractions are distractions to purpose, and a *mujahid* is disciplined and focused. Zaben's purpose was to raise support for the Palestinian cause and Hamas in particular. The enemy at the time was Israel, not America. The goal was liberating the occupied territories, not global jihad.

Before his second arrival in New York, Zaben had never been to a Western metropolis and was totally unaccustomed to urban lifestyles and culture. His only cultural experience thus far had been his childhood in Ramallah, and he was shocked by all the sights, sounds, and smells of a big city, especially at night. To start, there were bars everywhere. Women were walking by themselves wearing suggestive clothing. Music played loudly in the streets. To a good Muslim, this was all *haram*, or forbidden. Zaben did not want to become what he heard his brother, Yousef, had—a nominal Muslim, engaging in drinking alcohol and other vices—but Zaben had not been exposed to this degree of temptation before. Finding himself alone on his journey, he needed help and guidance from somewhere. This was the beginning of the test of his faith. He tried to be mindful of what his father had said. He prayed five times a day even when alone, reciting "*Allah akbar*" ("God is great"), "*Subhan il' aha*" ("God is pure"), and "*Hamduallah*" ("Praise be to God").

Zaben did not want to lose his way in a land of infidels, either by becoming undisciplined or unfocused. He wanted to find other believers, attend Jummah services and remain faithful to Allah. Zaben had a purpose in Allah, but still the sights and sounds of the city invaded his thoughts. If only his younger brother, Sayeed, had made the journey with him, it might have been easier. The proverb says, "Two are better than one, for if one falls the other will lift him up." Abdel, however, was sent by himself, and loneliness can make a mind wander.

Zaben moved into an apartment in Brooklyn on Stillwell Avenue, in the Coney Island section not far from Mermaid Avenue.[23] A generation earlier, Woody Guthrie had lived on Mermaid Avenue, but the times had changed and so had the neighborhood. Brooklyn was, so the sign says, the fourth largest city in the United States. It's a cornucopia of people, places, and events. Celebrities were born there, mobsters are buried there, and it's the place where "Da Bums" used to play baseball. Brooklynites are as diverse as the people buried in Brooklyn's Greenwood Cemetery. In that peaceful place, you can find people such as the esteemed newspaper editor Horace Greeley lying next to mobster "Crazy" Joe Gallo, along with Leonard Bernstein reposing in the same field as Boss Tweed.

Brooklyn is also known for what used to be a place of sun, sand, and fun: Coney Island. In the 1950s it was a poor man's vacation destination. People from all over New York City visited on holidays. Long before Disneyland existed, Coney Island had an amusement park called Steeplechase. There were the world-famous Cyclone and the Wonder Wheel, steam baths where old men turned to prunes, the boardwalk and penny arcades, and events like the Mermaid Parade and the Polar Bear Swim. There was always the smell of food cooking: hotdogs, french fries, corn on the cob, or knishes sold at a place called Nathan's. A family of five could eat for about two bucks. Above all, Coney Island had the ocean and the beach that offered—for the price of a subway token—a place to get away, relax, and unwind from the busy metropolitan life. It was a working man's paradise.

In the 1980s, however, it was ravaged by crack cocaine and violent crime. Housing projects and burned-out buildings replaced the amusement parks. Instead of gazing at girls in bathing suits strolling on the boardwalk, visitors looked over their shoulders to make sure there weren't muggers following them. The once-famous buildings were covered with graffiti and dirt. The stench of garbage hung in the air, and despair was on many faces. It was no longer a place where families wanted to go. If a family was stuck there, they were either desperately trying to get out or trying merely to survive.

This was the Coney Island Zaben saw, still suffering from the effects of the crime wave when he arrived late in 1990. It was gradually starting to change with a steady influx of immigrants to the area—immigrants who did not condone drug use or crime. These people had different customs, family traditions, and clothes. Once again, the place was no longer the Coney Island of the 1950s. Men and women wore, for example, shalwar kameezes, sarongs, kasekees, or burkahs. Many of the new immigrants were from the Far or Middle East, places such as Pakistan, Lebanon, and Yemen. Some were Sikhs, but many were Muslims, trying to make a living in a new country with new customs and new clothes.

Zaben was no different. He took to wearing a black leather motorcycle jacket and tight-fitting jeans. He slicked his hair back with pomade in an Elvis-style pompadour. This was the look of a greaser or wannabe gigolo, not a good Muslim brother. Even though he was attending Jummah services at various mosques, Zaben did not have the outward appearance of a fundamentalist Muslim, following the strict interpretation of the Koran. Why? The even more important question is, how did he balance his devotion to Islam with his outward appearance?

In Islam, whenever there is a question on belief or actions of a brother, an imam or clergyman may issue a *fatwa*, or religious ruling, that will help settle the discrepancy between belief and practice. The ruling by an Islamic scholar can grant exemptions from Islamic law to the follower when acting according to Allah's will. "Ibn Tamia—may Allah have mercy upon him—[is] said if a Muslim is in a combat or godless area, he is not obligated to have a different appearance from those around him. The [Muslim] man may prefer to look like them, providing his action brings a benefit . . . . learning their secrets and informing other Muslims. . . . Necessity permits the forbidden, even though [the forbidden acts] are . . . prohibited." This quote came from a page in a classified document originally called "The Manchester Document" but soon dubbed by the FBI as "The Al Qaeda Manual." A copy of the manual was found by the Manchester (UK) Metropolitan Police when searching an apartment of a known al Qaeda member.[24] It was on an individual's computer subfolder titled simply "military series," but in actuality it contained eighteen chapters on procedures to conduct jihad warfare. It also contained religious rulings by a noted Islamic cleric. This ruling allows a Muslim man to partake of all the debauchery he can, as long as he is doing it for the cause of Allah—sex, drugs, and rock 'n' roll without the guilt.

Years later, in a recorded conversation with a potential recruit, Zaben explained this religious dispensational ruling when asked about jihadists and the dress code. The recruit said, "They don't have beards . . . they should have let their beards grow. . . . [They] say, 'I joined the Jihad to die for the cause,' but they don't have a beard. It bothers me." Zaben replied, "Yes, some of the brothers go to places where it is dangerous. If they have a beard, they will be recognized. . . . [The jihadist] has to change the color of his hair and complexion until he goes to the target, so on and so forth. In Gaza and the West Bank right now if a young man has a beard he will be a target of the Israeli forces. This is the main reason. Allah knows why they don't wear a beard."[25]

Despite the fatwa, Zaben still had a conscience. He did not want to embarrass his family in Ramallah. What would his father and mother say if they found out he was drifting in a sea of unbelief? Soldiers often find it easier to maintain discipline on the battlefield than behind enemy lines. Thus it was for Zaben. The city seemed so decadent, so enticing—so many choices that he had never faced before.

New York City has always been a melting pot for different people, cultures, and religions, and most New Yorkers pride themselves on their ability to get along with each other. However, sometimes events occur that set one group against another, and violence erupts. Approximately six months after Zaben arrived in Brooklyn, Jewish writer and activist Meir Kahane was shot and killed while speaking in a New York hotel. Well known for his inflammatory rhetoric against Arabs, African Americans, and other minorities, Kahane had founded the Israeli political party Kach, which the State Department declared a terrorist group in 1994, several years after Kahane's murder. The police arrested a young Egyptian immigrant named El Sayyid Nosair and charged him with the crime. Animosity and tension between Arabs and Jews in the city rose during Nosair's trial. Nosair was found not guilty of the murder but was convicted on lesser charges, illegal possession of a handgun and assault. He received a sentence of seven to twenty-one years and was sent to the Attica Correctional Facility.

Less than a year later, on August 19, 1991, a seven-year-old boy, the son of Guyanese immigrants, was struck and killed by a station wagon driven by a Jewish man. The crowd that had gathered at the site of the accident set upon the driver and began beating him. During the melee, a young Orthodox Jewish student from Australia was stabbed by a sixteen-year-old African American youth and beaten by others as the crowd shouted, "Get the Jew! Kill the Jew!"[26] With that incident, the Crown Heights section of Brooklyn erupted into days of rioting, looting, and firebombing.

No one lives in a vacuum. People are shaped by the events surrounding them. In Zaben's mind this was exactly the same as being on the West Bank during the intifada. The enemy was the same. The means of action were the same. He was beginning to fit right in and feel at home.

Zaben had to support himself and decided to build a career in his new country, the Land of Opportunity. He thought about driving a cab, but to do that he would need a New York State driver's license. He quickly obtained one, citing a different address than his apartment on Stillwell Avenue. He used 443 68th Street, an apartment building off Fourth Avenue in Brooklyn. Once again, how did an illegal alien obtain a valid driver's license so easily? Or more important, why did Zaben use an address on Fourth Avenue and not his apartment in Coney Island?

Fourth Avenue stretches from one end of Brooklyn to the other, from the Verrazano-Narrows Bridge and Fort Hamilton to Atlantic Avenue and the Brooklyn Bridge. The New York City marathon runs right down Fourth Avenue. The subway runs directly underneath it right up to where the R train stops before beginning its run back over the bridge into Manhattan. The avenue bisects the borough. To be on Fourth Avenue in Brooklyn is to see the lifeblood of New York City up close. It is a main artery running through the body of the metropolis. Stand on it long enough, and you can hear the heartbeat of the city. Walking Fourth Avenue an observer can see a bit of everything: restaurants, bodegas, fruit stands, bakeries, apartment buildings, parks, and stores of all types—businesses that are owned, operated, and lived in by a conglomerate of ethnic groups: Chinese, Korean, Italian, Irish, Russian, Greek, Pakistani, Yemeni, and Mexican, among others. A person can buy cannoli, knishes, egg rolls, baklava, or mollete on the same street. You breathe it. You taste it. You feel it. Your finger is on the pulse.

There are also many places of worship representing various faiths along Fourth Avenue: churches, synagogues, and mosques. Among them is the Islamic Center of Bay Ridge. Zaben had many friends who attended this particular mosque. One of them, Basman Aziz, was a Palestinian immigrant who owned a furniture and carpet store on Fourth Avenue and 58th Street. Aziz, who will figure in Zaben's story later, lived on 74th Street in a beautiful house between Second and Third Avenues. Less than a hundred feet away from his home was another place where men of Middle Eastern descent came and went during all hours of the day and night. So significant was this address—265 74th Street—that in the summer of 1992, six months prior to the World Trade Center bombing, the FBI requested information from another governmental agency on both the phone activity and the people who frequented the house. In an attempt to identify a possible terrorist cell and prevent an attack, the agents were desperately seeking to identify anyone who had come or gone through that home.[27] One of those identified was the El Sayyid Nosair, who had been arrested for shooting Meir Kahane. At the time of the FBI's request for information about visitors to the house, Nosair was in Attica.

Not far from this street, again in Brooklyn, Zaben had another friend, Rashid Baz, who attended Jummah services with him at the mosque on Fourth Avenue. Baz was to become a significant figure in the jihad. For now, he was simply a cab driver. Zaben continued moving about Brooklyn to visit these Muslim brothers, navigating his way from house to house along the avenue until its end at Atlantic. Here, in the downtown section, there is a mosque called Al Farooq. Zaben often attended the same *masjid* where two of the most revered Muslim clerics had preached: Sheikh Muhammad Hassan, a fellow member of Hamas, and Omar Abdel Rahman, also known as the Blind Sheikh. There had been an upheaval with the clergy at that mosque. Those who were in disagreement with the teaching of the Blind Sheikh were forced out, including a Sudanese imam named Zakaria Gasmalla, who later became a New York Department of Correctional Services (NYDOCS) chaplain during the period Zaben was in prison.

If you left the Al Farooq mosque and headed east on Atlantic Avenue to Bedford Avenue, you would arrive at the Masjid Al Taqwa. The two are only a mile and a half apart. As you approached the mosque, one of the first things to catch your eye is the impressive rise of the structure. Next, you would notice the two massive gargoyles standing at the entrance to the building. At second glance, you realize that the gargoyles are in fact living, breathing men. Their heads, with their dark piercing eyes, rose out of huge chests. Their shoulders blended with their necks. Their faces lacked smiles or joy; they seemed devoid of emotion. Their eyes were constantly moving, scanning the crowd as it entered for Friday evening services. These sentinels guarded the imam from those who might seek to enter the *masjid* for reasons other than to pray.

These sentinels, or *sherters* as they are called, stood guard in the early 1990s and had impressive dossiers that added to their ominous appearance. Both spent more than five years in the penitentiary for vicious crimes of violence and had an extensive history of weapons possession and use. They had pledged allegiance to Allah and to the imam, promising to protect him with their lives, willing to lay them down if someone tried to invade the mosque and harm the teacher. Heretics who dared to challenge the imam's teaching would face their wrath. At the end of the service when the faithful gathered around in groups for discussions, they were closely monitored. The imam, Siraj Wahhaj, became the first Muslim cleric to open the U.S. Congress with prayer. Later he was known for his fiery sermons exhorting believers to jihad. Wahhaj was also later named as an unindicted coconspirator in the World Trade Center bombing of 1993.

Apart from the common gatherers, an inner group consisting of men known as the Talem Circle would discuss the security concerns of the Muslim community and dispense discipline to offenders where needed. No one entered this inner circle of the mosque without first going through the sentinels. These two men, Dawa and Edai, were well known throughout the Islamic community in New York City. Both were knowledgeable in Koranic, Salafi, and Wahhabi teachings, having learned it while incarcerated in the state prison. On more than one occasion, they gave the sermon when the imam was absent.

In these mosques in Brooklyn, Zaben also studied the Koran and the Salafi teachings of renowned Muslim clerics in an environment free from the invasion of what he perceived to be the enemies of Islam. At the time in the Islamic community in New York City, it seemed that there was no room for middle ground. The call went out to the faithful: "All you who believe take a stand for Allah and take a stand against the enemies of Allah." This was preached continually in the sermons that Zaben attended in Brooklyn.

Zaben enjoyed attending services at these *masjids* so much that later as a prisoner, he encouraged and directed future converts to go to

Jummah services there. More often than not, he helped in their conversion to Islam as they were eagerly anticipating release from prison.[28] In the early 1990s in New York City, Zaben was for all intents and purposes a devout Muslim, even if his appearance was not. He was praying daily, attending Jummah services on a regular basis, building relationships with other Muslim brothers and still in touch with his friends and relatives overseas. He even had gainful employment working for Ali Kased, a leader in PFLP, as a sales clerk.[29]

Despite all this, something mysterious started to change in his behavior. Zaben began committing kidnappings and armed robberies. He and another Arabic man purchased a cargo van and trolled Manhattan late at night looking for easy marks, waiting until they saw a person walking alone, preferably a man. They would then grab him, throw him into the back of the van, tie him up with duct tape, place a bag over his head, and take his wallet. They had obtained firearms from unknown contacts in the underbelly of the city and were willing to use them. Once they had the victim's credit cards, they put a gun to his head and demanded his PINs.

When the average person feels the cold steel of sudden death put to his or her head, the victim willingly and quickly gives up information. Having obtained the PINs and with their victim still tied up in the van, Zaben and his accomplice would drive around to an ATM and extract the person's funds. During the abductions, Zaben and his partner yelled back and forth in both Arabic and English. One night he was overheard by one of his victims saying about the money, "this is for the cause."[30]

After holding their terrified victims for five or six hours, they would release them on a dark, deserted street in the warehouse district. So traumatized was one victim that when interviewed about the incident ten years later, he broke down sobbing and shaking uncontrollably. Disoriented, scared, and utterly alone, the victim posed little threat to them. They had put the fear of Allah into the victims, telling them they knew where they lived and would kill them if they spoke to the authorities. This tactic worked until one of the victims was able to see the license plate of the van as it sped away. Dazed and still fearing for his life, he managed to call the police. And so, on January 26, 1993, New York City police officers arrested Abdel Nasser Zaben.

He was taken to a Midtown precinct and picked out of a lineup by one of the victims. A search of the van uncovered additional evidence of the abductions and robberies. The second suspect, Zaben's friend and accomplice, had worn a ski mask during the kidnappings. No accurate description of him was provided by the victims other than that he was a male speaking Arabic.

Zaben became just another prisoner in a crime-ridden city, waiting to be taken into the abyss.

CHAPTER 2

Changing Neighborhoods

The detective hammered away at the suspect: "You're facing a shitload of time, asshole! Tell us who he is, and it'll go easier for you. You don't owe him anything. Help yourself out. Do the right thing."

When criminals are arrested, especially for the first time, often they don't stop talking. They give up everybody. It's a bargaining process, a give-and-take between the suspect and the police. Forget "honor among thieves." They talk nonstop, like a running faucet. Sometimes the police interrogator is the first one to ask for a break during the "interview."

Whenever a person is questioned by the police about a crime for which he has been arrested, he is usually thinking both how to answer the questions and why the police are not asking about his other crimes—the ones he hasn't been arrested for yet. He'll fidget and sweat and unknowingly telegraph a message to the interrogator that he knows something that he's holding back. Usually, the cop's response is to keep pressure on him until he tells all. A good cop can often solve more than one crime with the right questioning. An interrogator could be talking to a petty thief, for example, who committed a breaking-and-entering misdemeanor and the thief will confess to a felony homicide. Major crimes have been solved this way. A common refrain among justice personnel is that whenever a crime is committed, either somebody in jail did it or knows who did.

But that was not the case with Zaben. In accordance with his Islamic faith and Sharia teaching, Zaben would not testify against another

Muslim. It is *haram* (forbidden). There is no fatwa for that. Because of his insistence in following his teaching, the other Arab male involved in the kidnappings with Zaben was never apprehended.

Following the fingerprinting and photographing of any criminal is the completion of the "61 form," standard paperwork filled out on everyone arrested by New York Police Department officers. Police must fill out the 61 in the precinct and give it an assigned number officially recording the arrest. A police officer or detective cannot take an arrestee to Central Booking without a 61 number. Filling out the form is part of the bureaucratic process of police work that can sometimes distract an officer from his main objective—solving the crime.

After the detectives completed this paperwork on Zaben's case, he was transported to Criminal Court in Lower Manhattan for arraignment. As far as anyone knows, this was the closest Zaben would ever get to the World Trade Center. After appearing before the judge for his arraignment, he was taken to his new residence, the New York City prison complex on Rikers Island. His journey through the American prison system had begun.

On February 26, 1993, thirty days to the date from when Zaben was arrested, a truck loaded with explosives was driven into the underground parking garage of the World Trade Center and detonated by an Arab male. The jihad had come to America.

The investigation into the first World Trade Center attack was conducted by various federal and local agencies—both jointly and separately—and was spread out over several years. It outlined a matrix of associations consisting of individuals and places that had been a part of Zaben's world. Several of the conspirators had attended Jummah services at the same mosques Zaben had frequented in Brooklyn.[1]

The address he used in Brooklyn for his driver's license—443 68th Street—was right next to the Islamic Center of Bay Ridge where his friend Rashid Baz and others went to Jummah services. There was also the apartment building at 265 74th Street in Brooklyn connected to the young Egyptian El Sayyid Nosair, who had been arrested for involvement in Kahane's shooting.[2] Even with these connections established, not one person came to question the twenty-three-year-old Arab man named Abdel Nasser Zaben imprisoned on Rikers Island. Zaben did not have to squirm or sweat about being questioned. Instead, he was learning about living in prison and trying to survive in his new environment.

"Survive" was the key word. In 1993, his home was the sprawling New York City Department of Corrections complex on Rikers Island, located just across the water from LaGuardia Airport. The only way onto the "Rock" is to drive over the bridge from Queens off Ditmars Boulevard onto Hazen Street. It is an enormous facility with numerous buildings for both men and women. At any given time, there are between 14,000 and 19,000 inmates there. During a single year, more than 110,000 inmates will pass through Rikers. That's a lot of people moving through the finite world of a prisoner. Not all are in the same situation. Some are serving sentences of one year or less. Some are sentenced to more than a year and are awaiting transfer upstate to the New York State prison system. Still others may be parole violators picked up for violating the conditions of their release. And some are pre-conviction arrestees, individuals awaiting trial or final determination on their legal proceedings.

On any given day, buses loaded with inmates are traveling back and forth from the New York City courts. For most convicts, that's the only way they will see their old stomping grounds—from the window of a prison bus. There is constant movement on or off the Rock. Inside, however, time and motion seem to stand still. In 1993 Rikers Island was a war zone—an environment with which Zaben was well acquainted, having spent his childhood on the West Bank during the intifada. But this war was different. The lines of demarcation were not so easily identified. This was a place where street rules applied, and he had to learn them. Gangs, such as the Latin Kings, Bloods, and Ñetas, exercised authority in the cellblocks. Racial division along the lines of black, Hispanic, and white was prevalent. Drugs were bartered and sold. Shanks (homemade knives) were the weapons of choice. Stabbings over something simple like using a phone that "belonged" to another group of inmates or showing disrespect to a fellow convict were common.

But in addition to learning how to survive, Zaben had to watch out for the guards. In 1993, a class action lawsuit was filed against the New York City Department of Corrections by a group of inmates alleging physical abuse by the guards. There were ongoing federal and city investigations into the violence and abuse against inmates in the Central Punitive Segregation Unit, also known as the Bing. New York City admitted to the abusive conditions but refused to indemnify the forty-three corrections officers and high-ranking officials named in the lawsuit. According to Howard Wilson, the New York City's investigation commissioner, there were "deliberate beatings . . . beatings planned and carried out by correction officers."[3] It seemed that even the guards lived by the law of the street: "payback is a mother——." With sayings such as "Get them before they get you" and "Cover your ass," the guards seemed to have forgotten the section in their employee manual in which they are encouraged to be "firm, fair, and consistent" in the treatment of all and that one of the goals of corrections is the "care" of inmates. Certainly, I am not saying that convicts need to be coddled. But if, as a corrections officer, I'm focused primarily on my survival and not on doing an honorable job as a public servant, then I will revert to the law of the jungle in my treatment of prisoners. This is what I believe had happened in 1993 among the staff on Rikers Island.

For the prisoners, with an ominous feeling of helplessness in their souls, it was a time when many sought answers outside themselves. It is said there are no atheists in foxholes or prisons. A lot of convicts find religion while locked up. Zaben already had Islam, but his faith grew deeper while he was inside. Through meetings with other Muslims in jail and the exhortation of his father and mother to remain true to the Prophet, he was pushed back to the fundamentals. He found most so-called Muslims in the city jail did not know how to read the Koran in the original Arabic, as many of them were Black Muslims, followers of Elijah Muhammad and the Nation of Islam. Zaben felt strongly that if they could not understand Arabic, they couldn't truly understand the Koran. He went to Jummah services in the jail mosque, met with the civilian imam, and spoke with the Muslim inmates about teaching them Arabic.

In meeting with the Rikers Muslim clergy, Zaben became acquainted with an eclectic group, to say the least. One chaplain was Malik-K, an African American who had been convicted of two armed robberies and associated with Jamaat al-Fuqra, a Black Muslim terrorist organization. Another was Abid-H, who had served time for a homicide. Yet another was Abdul ud-din-Bilal, who had amassed ten arrests going back to the early 1970s. The most serious of his charges was second-degree murder. These were the kind of employees overseeing the spiritual growth of Zaben and others on Rikers Island.[4] Their influence and his faith and fervency were growing at an alarming rate. Zaben was becoming a strong and faithful witness for Allah in the jail, sharing his beliefs with other inmates, seeking to convert them to Islam.

One of his first disciples was a young Puerto Rican man known as C-Low. He had been arrested in Queens in April 1993 for a brutal homicide and robbery and was sitting on the Rock facing a life sentence.[5] Only nineteen years old, he had been raised as a Roman Catholic in a dysfunctional and unstable family environment. He was impressionable, alienated, distressed, antisocial, angry toward authority, and obviously had a propensity for violence. In a nutshell, he had all the characteristics that made him a likely candidate for recruitment and indoctrination by terrorist organizations.

Unfortunately, law enforcement and intelligence experts would need more than ten years and millions of dollars to identify these general characteristics during a series of post-9/11 studies. Government agencies used psychologists, social behaviorists, and profilers, as well as forensic studies of known or captured terrorists—such as José Padilla and Richard Reid—to determine susceptibility. The findings were outlined in two classified documents that identified the characteristics an Islamic terrorist looks for in a potential recruit. The first, from the CIA, states,

> Prisons and the Internet provide easy access for radical imams to recruit lonely, angry adolescents to learn an anti-Western form of Islam. Incarcerated individuals are probably particularly receptive to using violence against a government by which they feel they have been wronged. In an apparent play on this psychological vulnerability, detainee and press reports indicate that imams from extremist groups are actively recruiting prisoners and those in disaffected, inner-city communities.[6]

The second, from the Federal Bureau of Investigation, states,

> The American prison system represents a sizeable pool of individuals vulnerable to radicalization. . . . Radical imams or volunteers can target a minority inmate's feeling of discrimination in the [United States] or perceived American oppression of minorities and Islam overseas. . . . Many inmates possess at least some of the characteristics that an extremist would desire, such as: hostility toward authority, particularly the U.S. government, longing for acceptance

> into a group for social interaction and/or protection, a violent predisposition, seeking power and influence, possibly to right the wrongs the inmate perceives he/she suffers.
>
> An additional concern is inmates radicalizing other inmates. Prison officials must be alert to the possibility of charismatic, religiously radical inmates spreading radicalization throughout the prison. Inmates incarcerated for crimes connected to terrorism or inmates with overseas religious instruction may possess extra credibility with other inmates, enough to gain a religious following inside the prison.[7]

Zaben recognized all this and more in C-Low the first day he walked into cellblock C-95, where they were both housed. They went to meals together. They went to the recreation yard together. They went to the visiting room together. They spent a lot of time in the same places, and Zaben made the most of every minute with C-Low.

Every day Zaben shared a passage from the Koran with him and encouraged him to go to Jummah services on Friday afternoons. C-Low had heard all the jailhouse raps, from the Nation of Islam guys to the Five Percenters. The Five Percenters belonged to the Five Percent Nation of Islam, a splinter group that was founded by Clarence 13X, a fellow minister with Malcolm X in the number 7 mosque in Harlem. Clarence 13X, who was murdered in 1969, believed in a mathematical equation of faith, that 85 percent of the population were totally ignorant of the truth, 10 percent of the people had some knowledge, and that the remaining 5 percent possessed complete knowledge of the truth. It was viewed by corrections administrators as a cult, a gang, or a racist sect, and they refused to recognize it or allow its members to congregate. Those who did were subject to disciplinary action. It was not until 2003 that a federal court ruled that it was a legitimate faith protected under the Constitution's first amendment.[8]

Zaben was different, not only in appearance but in behavior. Zaben was very cognizant of the importance of this. He knew exactly what he was doing as he demonstrated devotion to his faith not only by wearing a beard and a kufi but by praying five times a day in his cell, fully aware that others were watching. He refused to eat food that was not halal, such as pork. His calculated behavior commanded respect from the other inmates in the cellblock. Zaben would often come to

C-Low's cell before lock-in and teach him Arabic, continually speaking to him about Allah. He was discreet about these meetings, never embarrassing C-Low in front of other inmates. He would isolate him, catching him when he was by himself or depressed, then talk to him about being a Muslim and finding his purpose in the pages of the Koran. So good was the tutoring that C-Low soon became conversant in Arabic.

Zaben spent the greater part of a year together with C-Low teaching and preaching the way of Allah to him. And so it was, one day toward the end of their time together on Rikers Island, in the prison *masjid*, that C-Low made his *shahada*, his declaration of faith, repeating the words "*La ilaha-illa-llah, wa Muhammad rusulu-llah.*" ("There is no god but Allah, and Muhammad is the messenger of Allah.") C-Low did this publicly, in front of the other inmates. He was not ashamed. C-Low was Zaben's first convert within the prison system, but he would not be his last.[9] As a result of C-Low's conversion, Zaben was spurred on in this faith. He had finally found his purpose. Perhaps he could not take action against the unbelievers as some other good Muslim brothers had done, driving a truckload of explosives into the garage of the World Trade Center, but he could provide converts for the cause of Allah.

Some have called prison "the belly of the Beast." If that is true, then Rikers Island had become the womb where a single cell could take root and grow until it was ready to be born. After more than thirteen months there, Zaben reconnected with an individual he knew from the mosque in Brooklyn who was on Rikers awaiting trial. This was a fellow believer who had publicly demonstrated his faith in Allah, going so far as to kill those whom he said were the sworn enemies of Islam: the Jews. That individual was Rashid Baz, known as the Brooklyn Bridge Shooter, who had been arrested on March 2, 1994, for opening fire on a vanload of Hasidic students, wounding several and killing one.[10]

For this act, Hamas had awarded Baz the title "Mujahid Ibn Islam"—Holy Warrior and Son of Islam. The group went as far as distributing leaflets from Gaza describing his deeds. But despite his honored reputation, Baz was just another prisoner with Zaben, an inmate with whom he had a lot in common. Both had Palestinian mothers and had lived in Brooklyn and attended the same mosques. Both Zaben and Baz had a fervent desire to rid not only the West Bank but also the world of the "enemies of Islam." Their view was global; their actions were local. They both remembered the words of the sermons they had heard in the *masjids* in Brooklyn, and by Allah's will, they were together in jail. As it turned out, they would be together for a while, as Zaben was sentenced to eighteen years and Baz to one hundred and forty one. Their neighborhood was indeed starting to take shape.

Perhaps the sign on Interstate 84 about sixty miles north of New York City should have quoted Dante on Hell: "Abandon hope all ye who enter here," instead of simply stating, "Warning: Correctional Facility. Do Not Stop." In the town of Fishkill is the entrance to the New York Downstate Correctional Facility. It is the reception, classification, and diagnostic center for all convicted felons sentenced to the custody of NYDOCS. This facility is where the buses from Rikers Island and other city and county jails, carrying men who have been found guilty, unload their cargo. Being human cargo is only the beginning of the payment of their debt.

It is here that the prisoners, chained to each other and wearing civilian clothes for the last time, are ordered off the bus and marched into the reception center for processing. Here they are met by their keepers, the guards. To fearful eyes, the guards are not unlike Dante's monstrous character Charon, who stands in the vestibule of Hell about to take the dead to their punishment and shouts, "Woe to you depraved souls! Bury here and forever all hope." It was here on May 18, 1994, that Zaben arrived.

The first thing to hit Zaben as he exited the bus was the smell. It's a mixture of disinfectant, crossbar steel, and human stain that cannot be duplicated anywhere. The odor is not easy to describe to someone who hasn't experienced it, but it cannot be forgotten. It's as if someone combined the concepts of fear, despair, hatred, and loneliness with the physical realities of concrete and iron, then threw in some medicinal sanitizer like Betadine. It seems someone is always sweeping, mopping, and scrubbing in this 'hood, but that smell never goes away.

The next of Zaben's senses that adjusted were his eyes. One of the things that stood out in the prison complex was the shade of green. It's not the green of an emerald or a meadow or a tropical sea. There is no vibrancy to this color. It's the shade of a docile leaf, a pigment tone that has been neutered to evoke the feelings of compliance, tameness, and complacency.

Zaben then heard the sounds of his new world, best described as an organized symphonic confusion where the sounds of authority and discipline meet street slang, defiance, and vulgarity. These sounds combine to form some sort of dark humorous aria sung in its own language. They were sounds that Zaben would learn and become accustomed to hearing. When they ceased, when there was only silence within the prison's walls (or within the cellblock), then Zaben would learn that all hell was about to break loose.

Most of us are accustomed to routine in our daily lives. How we start our day, how we dress, the commute to work, the ride home, dinner and bed are all based on routine. It gives us a sense of comfort and security. For Zaben, this new residence went beyond routine. He walked to the same places, ate the same food, and went to sleep and woke up at the same hours as his fellow inmates. He was trapped in uniformity. This was the world Zaben marched into as the guards slammed his cell door shut the first fateful night. He was alone in a cell, no longer a pilgrim but a prisoner.

A typical American prison cell is an eight-by-ten mix of concrete and steel designed to confine the body and inhibit communication with others. A terrorist cell is the complete opposite. It provides the freedom to grow and the ability to communicate with others in the most austere environment. To be able to identify the creation of this type of cell, you have to be able to identify the environment in which it grows. If you know your turf, really know it—the sights, sounds, smells, and faces of it—you will be able to detect the slightest shift or change. This is the smallest unit in life—a single-cell organism. It's not a huge growth embolism, and it is rarely visible to the naked eye.

We also know it's the synergy of space, time, and particular cultures that form a specific locality; it's what makes one place different from another. They say you can never really go home again, or more specifically, it's not the same when you do return. Remove or change any of the key elements—space, time, or group of people —and that place you remembered so well has changed. Geography and synergy not withstanding, in New York City one block or one event can be the strict boundary line between your being in Times Square, Herald Square, or Hell's Kitchen. Similarly, prisons have neighborhoods within them that may change owing to synergy, only at a different pace. The space is always there, but time moves slower. Serving a twenty-five-year to life sentence is like standing still. No one is going anywhere. If a prisoner does go, it's because he has escaped, and he is brought back to start all over again.

Upon arrival at Downstate, inmates are examined, diagnosed, and classified through a series of tests to determine which prison they will be sent to. Medical exams, IQ testing, and psychological screenings are rendered, as well as security classification determined. Language skills and vocational needs are evaluated. Much of this analysis utilizes records from the inmate's past. According to Zaben's, he had received a high school diploma in Ramallah. His Beta IQ test resulted in a score of 67, which according to corrections psychologists displayed below average intelligence. His language proficiency test showed that he had an English oral proficiency of satisfactory, meaning he could communicate in English, although it was not his dominant language. Arabic was. His reading comprehension was set at a sixth-grade level and his math level at ninth grade.[11] Because of the low scores on these tests (which were arguably language biased), correctional officials did not recommend a rehabilitation program oriented toward education. Instead, owing to the violent nature of his criminal offenses, the prison counselor listed that Zaben had a high-priority need for an alternatives-to-violence program. During this time of classification, inmates had the opportunity to state their religious affiliation. Zaben stated that he was a Muslim.

In the 1970s and early 1980s, the Muslims in the prison mosque were overwhelmingly African American. These Muslims were seen as more disciplined and less disruptive than other inmate groups. In fact, after prison riots such as Attica in 1971 and Sing Sing in 1983, Muslim inmates were credited with having prevented additional deaths and injuries to the hostages.

In the mid-1980s and 1990s, however, there was an influx of foreign-born Muslims into the prison system. An intelligence report found that between April 1985 and December 2003, the number of U.S.-born inmates increased by 88 percent, and the number of foreign-born inmates increased by over 200 percent. Muslims included inmates from Afghanistan, Algeria, Bangladesh, Iran, Iraq, Lebanon, Libya, Morocco, Pakistan, Saudi Arabia, Sudan, Syria, and Yemen. Ironically, all of these countries have been of interest in the war on terrorism. Even some of the civilian imams were foreign born and foreign educated.

During this period of transition, at least two Muslim chaplains employed in the state prison system had been approved by Warith Deen

Umar. One of them was an African American named S. A. Khalifah who served as the director of the Islamic Society of North America (ISNA). ISNA is the oldest Islamic organization in the United States and has received extensive criticism of its ties to terrorist organizations or activities. One of its board members, Imam Siraj Wahhaj, was named as an unindicted coconspirator in the first World Trade Center Attack in 1993. Another board member, Basan Osman, was involved in an Islamic trust fund that was indicted for providing money and other material support to a Palestinian Islamic Jihad terrorist group. Because of these and additional alleged ISNA activities, the FBI has refused to certify ISNA as an endorsement body for Islamic chaplains hired by the Bureau of Prisons.[12]

In 2003 J. Michael Waller, a noted terrorism expert and an Annenberg Professor of International Communication at the Institute of World Politics, testified before the U.S. Senate on the role of ISNA, saying that he believed the organization was a front for a radical Wahhabi ideology that had its roots in the Muslim Brotherhood movement. Waller said he was speaking not as a theologian of Islam but as an expert in political warfare and terrorist groups.[13] Other counterterrorist organizations have voiced legitimate concerns regarding ISNA, saying it was "an organization seriously tainted with extremism."[14]

Another imam in the New York prison system at the time was Osama Alwahaidy. Alwahaidy was a Jordanian-born clergyman who in 2003 was indicted by the U.S. Attorney's Office in Syracuse for involvement in a fraudulent Islamic charitable foundation. At the time of Alwahaidy's arrest, his inmate assistant was Rashid Baz, the convicted Islamic jihadist and cellmate of Zaben. As Chaplain Alwahaidy's clerk, Baz was allowed access to computers, phones, and the names of all Muslim inmates in prison. He was also permitted by Alwahaidy to make unrestricted and unmonitored calls from the phone in his office. Interestingly, this is the same job that El Sayyid Nosair held when he conspired to blow up the World Trade Center in 1993.

All three of these individuals—Chaplain Alwahaidy, inmate Rashid Baz, and Abdel Nasser Zaben—shared Jordanian, Palestinian, and Hamas ties. All were fluent in Arabic and well versed in the Salafist view of the Koran. As a result, an unusual dynamic between foreign-born Muslim convicts and the African American Muslim convicts occurred in the operation of the prison mosques. The foreign-born Muslim inmates were acquainted with a more fundamentalist view of

Islam such as Wahhabism, which was in direct conflict with the Black Nationalist view held by many African American inmates. In the Wahhabi view of Islam, all things are related to the kingdom of Allah. There is no room for nationalism or for reparations by a country for wrongs suffered by a particular portion of its population. However, because the foreign-born Muslim inmates were fluent in Arabic, they were deferred to as the leaders or imams of the mosque, as they brought more legitimacy and a global view to the congregation. This changed the dynamics of the Muslims in the prison. They were encouraged to learn Arabic and read Arabic literature. Volunteers came from New York City mosques to the prisons, some of the same mosques frequented by El Sayyid Nosair, Rashid Baz, and the Blind Sheikh. What was being preached in the Muslim community outside the prison was now being taught in the mosques within.

After approximately six weeks in the Downstate facility, Zaben was transferred to the maximum-security prison, Auburn Correctional Facility, outside Syracuse in the Finger Lakes region of central New York. Built in 1816, Auburn is the oldest prison in New York. As such, it has a tremendous amount of history going back to the lockstep marching of convicts, which didn't end until the 1930s, and a period when a code of silence was enforced. Atop a building at the front of the prison is a statue of a Revolutionary War soldier nicknamed Copper John. Silently and reverently, he has watched all the changes in the American penological system over the years. Convicts leaving the institution often refer to their "bit" as the "time I worked for Copper John." As the soldier faces out from the entrance of the prison with his back to the yard, it is the ambition of inmates to look "Copper John" squarely in the face, a feat that can be done only from outside the prison walls.[15]

In the 1990s, Auburn prison was awash in drugs and corruption. The main focus of any investigating agency at the time was to control the sale and use of narcotics and the corrupting influence it had on the staff. Assaults on employees and inmates were on the rise and were tied directly to the drug problem. Prison Intelligence and Critical Incident Management were both highly focused on this issue, and the policy was to identify disruptive inmates and transfer them. As a result, inmates who were not disruptive or appeared compliant were overlooked.

Shortly after the first World Trade Center attack, another interesting phenomenon took place in Auburn. El Sayyid Nosair had been transferred from Attica into federal custody, along with the Blind Sheikh. This was common knowledge. What wasn't well known was that an eclectic group of inmates arrived in Auburn near the same time. Two were codefendants of Nosair and had helped him make phone calls from Attica to coconspirators in New York and New Jersey. In addition there were Yousef Saleh and Nophan Hamdan. Saleh, a Jordanian national who was serving a sentence of fifteen years to life for second-degree murder and arson, had been arrested in New York City in 1980 for the firebombing of a Jewish deli in the Bronx that killed two people. Hamdan, a Palestinian, was serving a sentence of twenty-five years to life for second-degree murder. He was arrested in 1979 in New York City for firebombing a building in Brooklyn, killing one person.

Still other inmates of note included Anthony Bottom, also known as Jalil Muntaquim, a Black Liberation Army member serving a life sentence for the shooting deaths of two New York City police officers; David Gilbert, a former Weather Underground leader serving a sentence of seventy-five years to life for the Brinks Robbery in Nyack, New York, in 1981 that resulted in the shooting deaths of two police officers and a Brinks guard; and Leroy Smithwick, a hit man for a narcotics organization. On July 13, 1980, Smithwick followed a rival dealer into an elevator in a building in New York City and put two bullets into his head. For that, he was sentenced to twenty years to life. Smithwick converted to Islam while incarcerated, and his particular skills were used by the Muslim community within the prison. He was an enforcer of Sharia law on any inmate who committed an infraction, and if a non-Muslim inmate threatened another Muslim inmate, Smithwick was sent to straighten it out.[16] Rounding out this group was Rashid Baz, the Brooklyn Bridge Shooter, a Lebanese national serving a sentence of 140 years to life, whom Zaben already knew. And there was the young Abdel Nasser Zaben himself, having recently arrived at Auburn by bus from the Downstate Correctional Facility.

With a group of inmates like this, the rehabilitative process had its work cut out. These were prisoners who had expertise in moving about the country through a series of safe houses, were proficient with explosives, and had ties to international money and resources. They also had fervent religious convictions that made them unafraid to die or to take a life. It was truly fertile ground for terrorist proselytizing and planning.

Although inmates were separated in Auburn by cellblocks and other controls, the one common meeting place for many of them was religious services. For the Muslim inmates, that meant Jummah services in the prison mosque. In the mosque they were encouraged to follow the five tenets of Islam, including charity. This was a problem to prison administrators. Money and prisoners never mix well. Even in the area of charitable donations, there had to be some sort of oversight whereby inmate financial transactions could be monitored and controlled to prevent corruption, fraud, and extortion.

Unfortunately, NYDOCS oversight of the monetary system for inmate donations was flawed, to say the least. The process was convoluted by numerous transaction codes that often did not clearly show where or why the money was sent out. Many charities, both religious and secular, receive donations from inmates. The risk is when a charity funnels the money to a terrorist organization, as some have done. The Al Kifah Refugee Fund in Brooklyn was one example, and this was not the only Islamic charitable organization receiving money from inmates. Prison security officials did not vet the organizations to which inmates sent money. Zaben, Baz, and the civilian chaplains who solicited Muslim inmates for contributions knew this. Often in the prison mosque was a stack of blank disbursement forms that an inmate was told simply to sign. He dare not refuse under penalty of Sharia law enforcement. The rest of the paperwork was filled out by the chaplain's clerk and submitted to the prison's business office. For the process to be completed properly, the inmate was supposed to take the form to a sergeant in the cellblock, who would then authorize it. The sergeant was to verify the inmate's identity and also that he was making this transaction of his own free will and not being extorted. In the case of Islamic charitable donations, this was not done. The chaplain took the forms filled out by his clerk and brought them directly to the business office. He also verified that the organization to which the donations were to be made was authentic and that the inmates wanted the money subtracted from their commissary accounts and forwarded to a certain address.

After all, who would question a cleric's integrity? The reason for the transaction was often so obscure that the officials could not differentiate among money sent home, purchases of items on an NYDOCS-approved list, and charitable donations. The checks sent to these suspicious organizations on behalf of the inmates were made out in the name of the State of New York, thus making it appear that the government was complicit in their support. Tracking exactly how much was sent to the numerous charities is difficult. To see a more accurate picture, consider that New York State Inmate Commissary Account System handles more than $25 million per year.[17]

Money was also received by the inmates from Islamic organizations and foundations such as the Graduate School of Islamic and Social Sciences in Virginia and as far away as Saudi Arabia. Literature came in from organizations sponsored by foreign countries espousing a strict fundamentalist interpretation of the Koran.[18] This literature was approved by the NYDOCS Media Review Committee, which included, of course, the prison imam, or someone from Chaplain Services. The committee also included a security supervisor of the rank of sergeant or above, and a supervisor from Administrative Services department.[19]

In prison, if "you need to get a message to your people and you don't trust the phone, a common practice is to use a visitor." During this time, Auburn was having its share of compromised visitors—those back from trips to the Middle East, Cuba, or New York City with messages and contacts for various inmates. The vast majority of these visitors were women, as they have historically had a significant role in the prison subculture and radicalism.[20] It was no different with Zaben. One of the most frequent visitors at this time to Zaben and his associates was a woman who had traveled to Cuba and met with Assata Shakur, also known as Joanne Chesimard. Chesimard was a member of the Black Liberation Army who was convicted of the shooting death of a New Jersey state trooper in 1973. In 1979 Chesimard staged a daring escape from a New Jersey state prison and fled to Cuba. She had been classified as a domestic terrorist by the FBI with a reward of $1 million listed for her capture. This visitor had also traveled to the Middle East and Israel to protest what some considered the illegal occupation of Palestinian land. Recorded phone conversations with inmates detailed her affiliation with various political and socially active groups, some of which were considered by law enforcement experts as radical or subversive in their methods. Since this woman had visited convicted domestic terrorists in prison and had also visited with a fugitive and codefendant of theirs, it would seem to some that she may have become a secure communications conduit between incarcerated terrorists and those still at large.[21]

Another woman who visited inmates in Auburn was Isabel Oviedo. She visited Saleh, who introduced her to Zaben. Not long after the introduction and initial visit, Oviedo and Zaben were married in the visiting room of Auburn prison by an imam from a Syracuse mosque. And as the women continued to visit, a whole new neighborhood within the prison started taking shape.

CHAPTER 3

Mommy Dearest

In the prison subculture, the relationship between incarcerated men and the women in their lives is an interesting phenomenon worth noting. Wives, girlfriends, sisters, and mothers have the ability to affect how an inmate does his time, because sometimes they are his most important link to the outside world. Within this circle of influence, the most significant person in a convict's life is often his mother. Girlfriends come and go. Wives often leave. But Mom, she'll always be there for you. Her support and approval is vital.

Sante and Kenneth Kimes were a mother-and-son team and had developed a reputation for worming their way into people's lives—exaggerating their importance or wealth in social gatherings and embellishing relationships with celebrities in order to gain access to their intended victims' assets to take what they could get. If that didn't work, Kenneth killed the victim at the direction of his mother. They would then move on to another town, city, or state to start the process all over again. They were violent grifters. So special was this mother-son bond that even after they were arrested and convicted in the brutal murder of an elderly New York socialite, Irene Silverman, and sent to prison, the relationship grew stronger.

In October 2000, Kenneth Kimes took a reporter hostage in the visiting room of Clinton Correctional Facility, a maximum-security prison in Dannemora, New York. He had only two demands for the hostage negotiators. The first was that his mother not be extradited to California to face an additional murder charge. The second was to talk to her on the phone. At the time of the hostage incident, Sante Kimes was an inmate at the Bedford Correctional Facility for Women in Westchester, New York, about three hundred miles from the prison where Kenneth was being held. Despite the distance, the influence of his mother was so strong that steel bars and prison walls could not break it. The incident finally ended when one of the negotiators, Vernon Fonda, was able to overpower Kenneth and take his weapon while a SWAT team rescued the reporter from harm.[1]

During the investigation of Abdel Zaben's recruitment cell, members of Operation Hades discovered another warped and bizarre mother-and-son scenario. This time, however, the evil influence came from the child.

Michael Lombard was a fifty-five-year-old Italian American born and raised in New York City, the only child of Nick and Marilyn Lombard. Raised as a devout Roman Catholic, he was a blessing to his mother and a disappointment to his father. During his formative years, he was loved and adored by his mother, Marilyn, while Nick beat him repeatedly. Michael was never good enough for Nick, never the son he wanted. One beating was so brutal that his skull and orbital socket were fractured, and his right eye was never the same. So severely traumatized was Lombard from this beating that he required psychological therapy, including medication, in order to return to school. He hated his father. He always, however, found acceptance with his mother. She did not want to lose him and would do anything for him, although she couldn't protect him from the beatings.

Because of the eye injury, Lombard required continuous medical care. He was seeing a specialist in Brooklyn for a series of treatments, including a minor surgery, when things started to go wrong. According to Lombard, the doctor botched a procedure, resulting in a significant loss of vision in the affected eye. Lombard argued with the doctor, but according to Lombard the problem was not rectified. Filled with frustration and rage, Lombard stalked his doctor repeatedly until he finally pulled out a gun and shot him. The doctor survived the shooting, and Lombard was arrested by the NYPD for attempted murder.[2]

In a later conversation with his mother, Lombard said that he believed the shooting had been justified because the doctor had "brutally raped" his eye. He reasoned that if a person were sexually assaulted and the victim shot the assailant, no jury would convict him, and that this situation was no different.[3] Needless to say, twelve of his peers didn't see it the same way. Marilyn was distraught. She loved her baby, would do anything for him, and didn't want to lose him, especially to prison for twenty-five years.

Lombard went upstate into the prison system, where he discovered he was a minority both racially and socially. He was white, weak, and had depended on his mother far too much. He had no prior criminal history to brag about and had difficulty fitting in with the rest of the inmates, who were overwhelmingly recidivists. He couldn't seek out prior crime partners who might have known him from the streets. But he did have Mom. For at least ten years while in prison, Lombard talked to one person on the phone and one person only: his mother. No girlfriends, no significant others, no close friends—just Mom. He called her twice a day—once in the morning and once at night. Their conversations covered everything from current events to politics, but would inevitably end up with Lombard's pending litigation. He was suing the state for a wrongful conviction and, ironically, medical malpractice. It seemed Lombard was constantly having a problem with his doctors, and in his view the doctor was always at fault. Lombard developed a racial hatred for the people in his past and could often be heard screaming, "That Jew bastard!" when talking about his former eye doctor. His anger festered, and the seed was sown.

During this time in prison, at his lowest and angriest point, Lombard met Abdel Zaben. They ended up as cellmates at Fishkill Correctional Facility in the mid-Hudson area of New York, where Zaben had been transferred. Zaben understood Lombard's feelings toward the Jewish doctor; after all, he had suffered under the same enemy. Zaben spoke of the strength of Allah to vanquish the enemy, the teachings of the Koran, and the closeness and camaraderie of good Muslim brothers.

As a result of Zaben's proselytizing, Michael Lombard—this white, Italian American Roman Catholic only-child, away from his mother for the first time in his life—converted to Islam while in prison. He made his *shahada* in the prison mosque and began wearing a kufi and carrying a Koran in the prison yard. It seemed he had received answers to all of his questions but one: how would his mother react?

Lombard shared his newfound faith with his mother when she came to visit him at prison the next weekend. During this visit he introduced her to Zaben, who also happened to be in the visiting room that day receiving a visit from his wife, Halima. Normal prison visiting room policy prohibits the practice of what they call "cross-visiting." In order for prison authorities to control the environment and prevent the smuggling of contraband, an inmate and his visitor are supposed to stay at their assigned table and not talk with other inmates or visitors. If the guards see cross-visiting, they give the inmate and the visitor a warning. If it occurs a second time, the visit is terminated. Like all things in prison, any rule can be bent, broken, or manipulated to the inmates' advantage. In this case, the inmate or his visitor can make a trip to the restroom. If the inmate knows the guard working the room, he may be able to convince the guard to seat his "associate" at the table next to him. But the most common method of bending this rule is to go to the vending machine area for food.

Inmates in prison are not allowed to touch money. In order to get something to eat or drink during a visit, they can send their visitor to the vending machine area. Inmates are supposed to stay out of that area but can walk their visitors up to a certain point. In many prisons that point is designated by a line painted on the floor with the words "No Inmates Allowed Beyond This Line." Thus, inmates will stand at that line and wait to help carry things back to their table. The vending machine area is also a social place where the visitors can meet and talk to each other, but that interaction needs to be extremely discreet. If a male visitor is caught talking to an inmate's lady, for example, it is taken as a sign of disrespect. After all, the visitor will be going home and the inmate remains locked up. The incident could start a riot in the visiting room or even lead to the visitor being killed.

It is, however, acceptable in prison subculture for female visitors to talk with each other. In New York City, they often meet at Columbus Circle, where NYDOCS-sponsored buses board passengers for visits to prisons throughout the state. Sitting together during long rides, the women have ample opportunity to talk. One visitor may be going to visit an inmate in Attica, while another visitor is going to Clinton. They now have a common bond and an extended chance to talk about their loved ones. With this knowledge of each other, they can now exchange messages. This is exactly how some inmates in different prisons, especially ones with radical agendas or criminal motives, use their mothers, wives, and girlfriends to pass information. The NYDOCS Office of Ministerial Services oversees the free bus service program, which travels throughout the state with hubs in all the major cities and covers all sixty-seven facilities.

Following their initial meeting in the prison visiting room, Marilyn Lombard and Halima Zaben rode home together to New York City. They talked about how difficult it was both to have their loved ones in prison and to make the journey upstate every week to visit. Halima was especially understanding of Marilyn's situation. And why wouldn't she be? Halima Zaben was a veteran of the prison visitor culture. She had been a part of it for quite some time.

Born Isabel Oviedo in the Dominican Republic in 1952, she had arrived in the United States in 1966, three years before Zaben was born. Oviedo moved into the Washington Heights section of New York City and shortly thereafter developed a relationship with a young Dominican man. They had three children together—two sons and a daughter. Oviedo's boyfriend went upstate for a drug charge, beginning her ongoing contact with the Prison Visitation Program. She had visited and taken phone calls from numerous inmates over the years, most of whom were serving long sentences for narcotics trafficking. Zaben was introduced to her by a fellow inmate, and after just two visits, on September 13, 1994, Abdel and Isabel were married. She then converted to Islam, took Halima as her Muslim name, and continued living in Washington Heights with her grown children. She became Abdel's vital link to the world outside prison walls, helping him facilitate three-way phone calls with contacts in New York, Texas, Florida, and the Middle East. If necessary, Halima helped him by personally carrying messages to individuals when phones could not be trusted. Abdel's associates outside the prison walls were well acquainted with Halima. She became their faithful contact and Abdel's messenger.[4]

This system of communication came as no surprise to the counterterrorism experts with Operation Hades who had studied the al Qaeda manual. The manual advises its members who are in prison to use visitors to communicate with members outside prison.[5]

After the initial ride home, Halima and Marilyn exchanged phone numbers and addresses and saw each other often over the course of time. While Abdel worked on Michael Lombard's discipleship inside the prison, he had Halima invite Marilyn to Jummah services at a mosque in Brooklyn, the same one that he and others of like faith had frequented before they were incarcerated. And so things were being changed, little by little.

After a short period of time meeting with Halima, attending the mosque services, and talking to Lombard on the phone twice a day,

Marilyn was ready to make her *shahada*. Was it a true conversion, or was it an overwhelming desire to stay close to her son that caused her to change religions? That answer would come as she shouted, "*Allah akbar, jihad, jihad!*" ("God is great, jihad, jihad!") on the tape-recorded inmate telephone system as she had her daily conversation with Michael. The automated voice recording started, "This is the MCI operator, you have a collect call from, 'Hello, my name is Michael Lombard.'" There was a slight pause, then a clicking sound verifying the acceptance of charges and the connection, followed by the unmistakable exchange of greetings: "*Hamduallah* [Praise to Allah], Mother." She responded, "*Hamduallah*, Michael." With those words the dual diatribe started between mother and son.

The conversation continued with, "It's the Jews, Michael, it's the Jews—they control everything," and moved downward to Michael responding, "Bush is a puppet of the Zionists. Remember, Mother, you're *mujahid*, a holy warrior. We will win this battle. Allah will triumph over the enemies. There shall be a reckoning. I assure you, there shall be a reckoning. . . . Have a good night. Get your rest. I'm going to bed now, and I hope to dream of a large mushroom salad covering the city."[6]

Investigators realized that the "mushroom salad" that Lombard was speaking about was a nuclear device being detonated in the New York City metropolitan area. Everyone has a dream in life. That was Michael's. His and Marilyn's conversations contain the most vile anti-Semitic words ever to be heard between a mother and a child. They were spoken while the son was standing in a phone booth in the prison cellblock and the mother was sitting in an apartment in the Bensonhurst section of Brooklyn. While this was happening, the elderly husband and father, Nick, was lying in a hospital bed in the living room of the apartment. Occasionally, the recorded tapes caught the sound of him moaning in the background. He was dying of cancer, but Michael did not talk to him.

Marilyn, a frail, grandmotherly looking Italian American, had become, by her own concession and by her son's encouragement, a *mujahid*. It was like an odd Greek tragedy or a fictional story. If it weren't so tragic, it would be almost comical. Yet she had become the perfect pawn. In her conversations, often with Lombard's support and prompting, Marilyn spoke of her willingness to become a *shadeeda*. The word *shadeed* is Arabic for martyr, and in Islam it refers to a man who gives his life for the cause of Allah. A woman who does the same is called a *shadeeda*. Primarily, this person gives her life in the form of a suicide bombing, which has been a controversial issue in the Islamic faith. On the one hand, suicide is *haram*, but if in the process you take the lives of the enemies of Islam, you are not only accepted but are granted honor, according to some interpretations.

It was generally accepted for a man to become a *shadeed*. According to Ahmed Yassin, the religious founder of Hamas, a woman was to become a *shadeeda* only in special circumstances. Sheikh Yassin believed that a woman could only become a *shadeeda* if she was in fact atoning for some sin or transgression she had committed in her life (for example, if she had been promiscuous or had in some way dishonored her family). It was then acceptable to use this method to not only gain access to Paradise but to also restore the honor lost.[7] Knowing the facts of Lombard's family background, one can easily wonder if Marilyn carried a tremendous load of guilt for all that had happened in Michael's life, from child abuse to imprisonment. Had this been her failure?

Two years before the Republican National Convention was held in New York City in 2004, counterterrorism experts began to look at the possibility of a terrorist act of jihad during an election or a political event. Various hypothetical scenarios were discussed as to the methodology of the attack and the possible profile of the attacker or attackers. Mock training exercises for law enforcement were conducted and then evaluated. But there is nothing like real-time, live instances to prove the mettle of the man or the plan. As it turned out, one of the results of the diligence of investigators in Operation Hades provided officials with just that incident.

In October 2002, approximately four weeks before the November 5 elections, members of Operation Hades intercepted a telephone conversation between Michael Lombard and his mother. In it, they talked about an upcoming visit to New York City by then governor George Pataki. The governor was meeting with another government official, Dov Hikind, an Orthodox Jew, previously associated with Meir Kahane, who represented Brooklyn's 48th District in the New York State Assembly. At one point in the recorded conversation, Michael assailed the governor as a "puppet of Zionism," and his mother stated she wished Pataki dead. She also vaguely alluded to being willing to help kill him. After all, who would ever suspect an old woman in the crowd of being a jihadist?[8] The threat was deemed significant enough for the lead to be passed on to the governor's bodyguards. Following that, twenty-four-hour surveillance was placed on Marilyn Lombard and other associates of Zaben until after the governor's visit. Additional security measures were also taken, limiting crowd access to Governor Pataki and Representative Hikind during the event. Officials concluded that although no actual violent act took place, the potential had been real.

The reality of women as suicide bombers was demonstrated in March 2010 when Islamic terrorists from Chechnya detonated two explosive devices in the subway in Moscow, killing thirty-five people and wounding over a hundred others. The bombers were tentatively identified as female Chechen rebels from an offshoot Islamic group called Caucasus Caliphate Jihad. Russian authorities dubbed the female bombers Black Widows.

The incident had a worldwide ripple effect in the arena of counterterrorism measures. Alerts were issued both in Washington and New York City regarding the potential danger of female suicide bombers. The alerts described the ability of female attackers to move about and gain access to vulnerable areas more freely than men.[9] This warning came nine years after investigators from Operation Hades identified the threat of female jihadists in the war on terrorism. To be sure, Marilyn Lombard was not the first woman to voice a willingness to die for the cause of Islam. But it did give counterterrorism analysts a template for a woman's progression from convert to potential homegrown terrorist, in this case willing to do anything for her son, even die in the name of Allah. Knowing he has that commitment from his family sustains a jihadist while incarcerated.

So what does a prisoner do if he does not have the contact and support of his mother while he's locked up? "Gino" went to prison for the first time when he was nineteen years old.[10] He was a handsome, young Hispanic man with green eyes and a disarming smile. Putting a young man like that in prison is like throwing fresh meat into a pool of sharks; everyone will try to take a bite out of his ass. He couldn't possibly survive on his own. He needed a group to accept and protect him. Unfortunately, looking for acceptance was nothing new to Gino; he had sought it for years from his mother and never found it.

Gino was born in New York City to a drug-addicted prostitute. She was too busy doing business to give him the time, attention, and affection that a young child needs. He also had learning disabilities and never quite fit into the educational system, so he dropped out and ran the streets. Given these circumstances, Gino grew up as society would expect. He hooked up with a group of wannabe gangbangers in Richmond County doing bunco thefts and assaults. In 2001, he was arrested in Staten Island for criminal possession of a weapon, grand larceny, and burglary. On 9/11, Gino was sitting in a prison cell on Rikers Island waiting for his case to be adjudicated. He was a lost soul adrift in a sea of ignorance without meaning or purpose to his life. But the furthest thing from his mind was jihad. He was trying to figure out how he was going to survive in the Beast and was contemplating taking a plea bargain that would reduce his time but still give him four years in state prison. During the time he was waiting to go upstate, his mother never came to see him.

Gino was a textbook case for recruitment to a terrorist cell—a prime candidate for a homegrown jihadist. He had tried to gain acceptance with the Bloods, but he couldn't even pass initiation, as he wasn't smart enough to follow their instructions. According to a secret CIA/FBI profiling communiqué describing the four-step path for becoming involved with Islamic extremism, the first step for any recruit is to search for a new way of life that offers a sense of meaning and belonging. Then, in May 2002 Gino met Abdel Zaben at Fishkill. Zaben offered him acceptance "in the name of Allah, the Compassionate and the Merciful." During his time with Zaben, Gino completed the next two steps in textbook order: conversion to Islam and indoctrination in radical Islamic ideology.

Moving forward, he was now Abdul Alim Inshallah, a new name for a new identity and a new life.[11] Zaben continued his discipleship with Gino by instructing him in the Koran and teaching him Arabic. He encouraged him to continue his Islamic studies when he left prison by attending an Islamic school in Virginia and then possibly moving to the Middle East for further studies. Zaben assured Gino that he had helped other Muslim brothers released from prison by sending them both to the school in Virginia and overseas for training.

Gino was excited about his new friend, his new faith, and his plans. But despite all of this, he still craved acceptance from his mother. He called her constantly from prison. She would not accept his collect calls. She was moving on with her life; it didn't include him. She was no longer a prostitute but was now in a relationship with another woman and the two of them were planning to live together in an apartment in New York. Zaben told Gino that homosexuality was *haram* and that his mother needed to repent and convert to Islam. He also told Gino that his family may not accept his conversion, but he must be strong and endure these rejections, remembering that he is accepted by Allah and his Muslim brothers.

Gino wanted his mother to know what had happened to him in prison. He wanted to talk with her and share his faith. He had hopes that she might too become Muslim, and they could finally be a family, a real family in Allah. He desperately needed to talk to her. Finally, Gino convinced another inmate to help him bypass the prison phone system by making a noncollect, three-way call to his mother. Unbeknownst to Gino, the person helping with the call was an undercover operative for the NYPD Intelligence Division. Suspicions had risen regarding Zaben's associates, so the call was recorded. Gino began by telling his mother that he had become a Muslim and his name was now Abdul Alim. She laughed at him. He then went on to tell her about his studies in Arabic and his plans to travel and continue his Islamic studies when he was released from prison. She again ridiculed him, telling him his name would always be Gino, not Abdul or anything else anyone called him in the Joint. Every time he tried to say something, she would interrupt him with a derogatory remark. Exasperated after about twenty minutes of this, Gino started crying and yelling, "Why don't you listen to me? You never listen to me! You never hear what I'm saying!"[12]

When Gino went back to his cell, he told Zaben what had happened. Zaben quickly encouraged him and assured him that Allah and the true believers in Islam would always love and accept him. They would never ridicule him. Only unbelievers ridicule Islam—infidels, he called them. They are your true enemies.

The role of women, in particular the importance of the mother-child relationship as it relates to a terrorist or potential terrorist, has been well researched and documented by counterterrorism experts. Anat Berko, a former lieutenant colonel in the Israel Defense Forces, has written extensively on the psychological profile of suicide bombers in the Middle East. While writing her thesis for her doctorate in criminology, Berko interviewed numerous terrorists in prison as well as the spiritual leader and cofounder of Hamas, Sheikh Ahmed Yassin. In her book *The Path to Paradise*, she spoke of this phenomenon:

> The mother is the most significant figure for . . . the suicide bomber. . . . Many of them have no father figure. . . . Any conversation about their mothers causes a great rush of emotion and usually makes them cry.[13]

And so it was with Gino. A son's love, once rejected by a mother, can turn to hatred in the blink of an eye when the enemy is finally identified. Thus Gino entered path number four in the CIA/FBI profiling communiqué: participation in jihadi violence. The report notes that "some individuals, particularly those who convert in prison, may be attracted to jihadi violence . . . for [them] it represents an . . . outlet."

Left unchecked, Gino was starting to look for that outlet. It was at that point in the recruitment process that Zaben told Gino he had someone he wanted him to talk with. He introduced him to one of his prize pupils, a former inmate who after his release from prison and with the help of Zaben had been through the Islamic school in Florida and to several Middle Eastern madrassas for training. The former inmate was now known as Assad, the Lion.[14]

CHAPTER 4

The Lamb Becomes a Lion

Two years after Abdel Nasser Zaben entered state-run Auburn Correctional Facility, he was moved to a different location within the New York State prison system, mainly based on his good behavior but also because of the needs of the Department of Correctional Services. Zaben had not done any of what problematic inmates generally do—assaulted a guard, smuggled drugs, or tried to escape. As a result, he was reclassified according to NYDOCS guidelines from a maximum-security threat level down to medium security. In any case, since NYDOCS was experiencing a shortage of maximum-security cells, it relaxed the security guidelines to allow for a greater number of inmates to move to the newly constructed medium-security prisons. The NYDOCS budget was approaching $2 billion annually, and it was less expensive to keep an inmate in a medium-security environment. Furthermore, the concept of using frequent inmate movement as a management tool has long been a part of corrections.

On May 24, 1996, Zaben was transported about twenty miles south of Auburn down a country road to the Cayuga Correctional Facility. Situated in the Finger Lakes region of New York State at the tip of Owasco Lake, Cayuga is on 144 acres near the town of Moravia. The acreage was beautiful pastoral land that had primarily been used for farming. The prison was built in 1987 during the increase in convictions resulting from the 1980s crack epidemic. The engineering design of this prison is referred to as a cookie cutter. It was a prototype designed to facilitate rapid construction of desperately needed space throughout the New York State prison system.

As a medium-security prison it consisted of dormitory-style housing. The only cells in the prison at the time were limited to the thirty-two-cell disciplinary section called the Special Housing Unit, where inmates were confined twenty-three hours a day. In jailhouse slang, it was known as the Box. The name goes back in the history of prisons to when unruly convicts were placed in an actual six-by-six-feet box out in the sun as punitive discipline.

In addition to the dormitory buildings, there was an administration building, a vocational school building, a gymnasium/recreation building with a recreation yard and an infirmary building. If there weren't the double-link fences with sensors, cameras, and razor wire, it might look like a small college campus. From an economic point of view, the cookie-cutter design is very good. From a security point of view, it is questionable. The problem with this type of physical structure as a prison has been demonstrated during riots. Cookie cutters lack the cells and cellblocks of conventional prisons that can be sectioned off with control gates to prevent disruptive inmates from taking over the entire complex. Inmates can run amok with security standing outside the fence watching. Cookie cutters' aesthetically appealing exteriors are meant to reduce the prison's visual presence to tourists visiting the area and locals who live there year round. People go to the country to see mountain vistas and serene lake shores, not prisons. Nobody wanted to see an Attica-like fortress ominously protruding out of this panoramic vacation-land.

While Zaben was in this bucolic setting, he had the opportunity to meet a lot of inmates. At the time he arrived at Cayuga, the total number of convicts was approximately 1,300. Since it was a medium-security prison, inmates had a greater freedom of movement throughout their day, which included time to attend such programs as adult basic education, General Equivalency Diploma (GED), and vocational training in computers, masonry, and horticulture.

Zaben went about establishing a daily routine and in doing that made deliberate contact with the other convicts. He met them in the normal course of serving his sentence, sometimes in the mess hall, the yard, his dormitory, or his program assignment area. Several of the inmates he knew from his time at Auburn. One was Leroy Smithwick, the former drug hit man and Sharia enforcer. Smithwick had arrived about six months before Zaben and had already established himself in the prison yard and, more important, the prison mosque. He also held a job in the prison mess hall and saw virtually every inmate in the prison on a daily basis. For Zaben, this was strategic. Upon his arrival, one of the first faces he wanted to see was *ikhwan al muslimeen*, a Muslim brother. Smithwick took Zaben around the yard introducing him to all the fellow Sunni believers, providing him with the breakdown of who was strong and who was weak in their commitment to Allah. Smithwick also told the civilian imam and brothers in the mosque during Jummah services who Zaben was and where he came from.

Zaben was not the only inmate from the Middle East in Cayuga at that time. Kassem Al Shoaibi, a former colonel in the Yemeni army, was serving a sentence of six to nineteen years for a murder committed in the Buffalo area. Al Shoaibi was no one to be trifled with. Having grown up in the land of Osama bin Laden's ancestry, which is to this day an enclave of fierce *mujahideen* and jihadists, Al Shoaibi was intimately familiar with radical Islam. Yet despite his background, he feared Zaben. He told the counterterrorism investigators who were debriefing him that "Zaben is a real terrorist." He also spoke to investigators about Zaben's direct ties to radical Islamic terrorist organizations abroad and that Zaben was a member of Hamas.[1] It is not hard to imagine the stature to which Zaben rose in the Cayuga prison. On the one hand, he had an African American Muslim leader, Smithwick, who had spent long years in the prison system and carried a reputation as an enforcer, telling the inmates, "You better listen to this guy." On the other hand, a compatriot from the Middle East and fellow Muslim was telling the inmates, "You better fear this guy." Zaben had achieved rock star status before he had even begun to seek disciples. Inmates were flocking to him. If you were his friend, no other inmate was going to mess with you.

Among those Zaben met was a young African American named Edwin Lorenzo Lemmons, who arrived at Cayuga about a month before him. Lemmons was five years younger than Zaben, and like Zaben he was in the state prison system for the first time. Perhaps it was this factor that drew them together, or he could have heard of Zaben's reputation. Most likely Zaben saw another disenfranchised, alienated young man looking for a sense of purpose and belonging in his life and sized up another potential convert, as he had done in the case of C-Low on Rikers Island.

Lemmons was born in Chicago in 1974 to Jehovah Witnesses who sometimes would take him with them door to door as they spread the message of the Kingdom. As he approached his teenage years in the inner city, he developed some social and disciplinary problems. Wanting to eliminate young Lemmons's exposure to street gangs, drugs, and crime prevalent during the 1980s in Chicago, his parents shipped him off to live with relatives in Fulton, a rural town in upstate New York.[2] In its heyday, the historic Erie Canal, which flows right through Fulton, brought tremendous financial prosperity to the cities located along its route. But time changes people and places, and Fulton was no exception to the rule. By the time Lemmons arrived in Fulton, it was no longer prosperous.

Fulton had a population of about 11,000 people, of whom approximately 96 percent were white. African Americans, like Lemmons, made up less than 7/10 of 1 percent of the populace. Lemmons attended the local high school but only managed to complete eleventh grade. During this time, he began drinking, smoking marijuana, and getting into trouble with the local authorities. There was not much economic hope in Fulton for a young black man with a limited education. His first arrest came at the age of nineteen. During the next twenty-four months he was arrested four more times, for DWI, burglary, and assault. In May 1995 Lemmons was arrested for robbery in the first degree, a violent felony offense.[3] His conviction landed him in the Oswego County Jail, from which he was released to await trial.

In January 1996 Lemmons agreed to plead guilty to a lesser charge of attempted robbery in the second degree. In exchange, he was given an indeterminate sentence of two to four years in state prison. This meant that he could be released in two years if he exhibited good behavior, or he could stay as long as four years if he incurred serious disciplinary charges. With his hands in the fate of the powerful State Parole Board—or in prison slang, "the Pilgrims"—Lemmons was transferred in April 1996 from the Oswego County Jail to the custody of NYDOCS, yet another young black man entering through the Gates of Hades.

During his initial time in the Diagnostic and Reception Classification Center, he was examined for physical, mental, and educational health and needs. He declared his religion as Christian. A questionable reception assessment noted that his crime was not alcohol related, even though his Michigan Alcohol Screening Test indicated a significant substance abuse problem.[4] He was recommended for a vocational training program but not substance abuse treatment. As a result of his counselor's assessment, Lemmons's program needs, and more important the NYDOCS Classification and Movement criteria at the time, Lemmons was transferred to the medium-security Cayuga Correctional Facility.

By the time Lemmons met Zaben, Zaben's sphere of influence included the civilian chaplain, Saad Sahraoui. Imam Sahraoui was an Algerian national who had been hired in 1992 by the NYDOCS director of ministerial services, Warith Deen Umar, and assigned to Cayuga. Sahraoui was listed as a member of the Islamic Correctional Foundation of America and the Majlis of Central New York.[5] He also made trips back to the Middle East and North Africa during his period of employment.

Sahraoui was certified by the National Association of Muslim Chaplains, of which Umar was the founder and president. Umar selected all the imams to be hired by NYDOCS at the time. The philosophy that guided him when hiring Muslim chaplains was simple. He himself was trained as a Wahhabi Sunni Muslim, thanks to the Saudi government. It was therefore incumbent that all of the Muslim chaplains he hired subscribe to a Sunni/Salafi ideology. A Salafi is a person who was one of the early followers of Muhammad. The term has come to be associated with an orthodox or fundamentalist version of Islam and with the Muslims who adhere to a strict and literal interpretation of the Koran. Emphasis is placed on the Arabic roots of the religion, its leader, and the language of the Koran. In addition to his ecclesiastical endorsement from a certifying body, Saad Sahraoui received an even weightier one when Zaben told other inmates that Imam Sahraoui was a "good Muslim brother." They knew exactly what he meant: "He's one of us, a committed Wahhabi Salafist." Those civilian Muslim chaplains who were not fluent in Arabic often deferred to an inmate to lead the prison congregation in worship. When the chaplain was foreign-born—in this case Algerian, fluent in Arabic, and educated in Saudi Arabia—an even stronger alliance was built with inmates of like culture. This is precisely how Zaben, a native of the Middle East and fluent in Arabic, rose to the top of the Islamic community at Cayuga.

If you want to be a good Muslim you must study the Koran. To properly understand the Koran you must study Arabic. To learn Arabic you must have a competent tutor. Zaben once again stepped up and initiated a class in Arabic for those inmates at Cayuga who wished to learn the language of the Koran, which was taught in the prison mosque as a volunteer program. So it would not interfere with the prisoners' required program assignments, the class required an employee to endorse it for approval by prison administrators. Imam Sahraoui sanctioned the program.

Edwin Lemmons signed up for the course. It must have been a very good one, because several years later, government translators listening to intercepted telephone calls from him in Egypt remarked that his skill in the language was more than adequate and even used the word "scholarly" to describe his mastery of it.

It was in Cayuga Correctional Facility, under the teaching and discipleship of Zaben, that Lemmons made his conversion. He was given the name Assad Asaalam, meaning the "Lion of Peace." How genuine was Lemmons's conversion? He did ask that his records be updated to indicate the change of religion. He also requested a change in program assignment. After having successfully completed vocational courses in small engine repair and electrical training, he went before the program committee, a panel consisting of a security staff member, a program supervisor, and an administrator. The committee was supposed to review the inmate's background, the facility's needs, and the impact on security, if any, prior to a job assignment. In reality what would frequently happen was that a facility employee (in this case the chaplain) would go to the deputy superintendent of programs or the director prior to the inmate appearing before the panel and request that a particular inmate work for him. In that case all the committee does is rubber-stamp the assignment. Based on the recommendation of Sahraoui, Lemmons was assigned to the Chaplain Services Program. For the next twelve months, he was the imam's personal assistant, following in the footsteps of El Sayyid Nosair, Rashid Baz, and Abdel Zaben.

"Mustafa" is an African American born in 1963. A convicted narcotics trafficker, he has spent a considerable amount of his adult life incarcerated. He was a Muslim prior to going to prison, but his faith and commitment had been, at best, nominal. He told investigators in a confidential interview that when he went to prison, two inmates dominated Islamic discipleship. One was Edwin Lemmons and the other was Abdel Nasser Zaben. He met them both while at Cayuga. The three became close friends not only when attending the prison mosque but also in sharing intimate details about their lives. Mustafa said that when he first met Zaben, he was shown photos of him wearing military fatigues and brandishing weapons. The photos were taken in the Middle East prior to Zaben's imprisonment in 1993. Somehow he had managed to smuggle them in either by a visitor, a lax security guard, or a sympathetic employee, because photos of weapons were prohibited in the prison. The photos were used to bolster Zaben's already established reputation as a committed Islamic warrior. Zaben also told Mustafa that he was a member of an Islamic jihadist group that was willing to die for Allah. So now investigators had both Zaben's admission to Mustafa and the additional statement from the former Yemeni colonel, Al Shoaibi, that Zaben was a member of Hamas.

Mustafa spent more than a year together with Zaben and Lemmons at Cayuga before Zaben was transferred to Fishkill Correctional Facility. Mustafa remained at Cayuga with Lemmons for another year before Lemmons was released. The three remained in close communication through letters, visits, and phone calls. After he was released in October 2000, Mustafa received collect calls from Zaben in prison, and then he would place three-way calls to Palestine, Yemen, and Egypt. The conversations were always in Arabic. When Lemmons attended the Al-Aksar mosque in Egypt in March 2000, then went to Saudi Arabia for religious training, Mustafa continued communication with him. According to Mustafa, Lemmons also received "underground defensive training" while he was in the Middle East. He believes that training took place somewhere in Yemen where Zaben told him he had family.

Mustafa himself received an invitation from Zaben to go to Palestine and Egypt for training, but he declined and fell into old habits of dealing narcotics in the mid-Hudson area. Ashamed, he hid his criminal activity from both Zaben and Lemmons, telling them that he was still a good Muslim attending Jummah services and avoiding what was *haram*. They continued to talk to him about the recruitment efforts and contacts in detail until he was again arrested for dealing and placed in the Dutchess County Jail. At that time, Zaben was upset with the broken contact and persistently attempted to get in touch with him. He made numerous calls from both the inmate phones and the chaplain's phone to Mustafa's family asking to speak with him. Mustafa's family simply said he was not around. They were under specific instructions from him not to tell Zaben that he had been arrested and jailed. Trying another tack, Zaben requested that Lemmons attempt to contact him. Lemmons, too, was unsuccessful.

Zaben finally sent his wife to get the details of where Mustafa was and find out what if anything had happened to him. Halima was the one who informed Zaben that Mustafa was in jail awaiting trial. Immediately after receiving that news, authorities recorded a series of conversations between Zaben and Lemmons. In them, the two men expressed grave concerns that Mustafa, whom they referred to as their brother, might be talking with the authorities. Their concerns were well founded. He was indeed talking to the authorities, and his information was deemed credible by the investigators of Operation Hades in 2003.[6]

On September 14, 1998, Edwin Lemmons, aka Assad Asaalam, was conditionally released from Cayuga Correctional Facility. He was under parole supervision, meaning that his movements would be carefully scrutinized by the New York State Division of Parole. Lemmons immediately requested to have his parole transferred to the state of Florida and the city of Gainesville, where he would be living with an uncle. He also said he would be attending the Islamic Center of Gainesville to further his studies. The transfer was granted with the dual approval of the New York State Division of Parole and the State of Florida.[7] While living in Florida, Lemmons continued to maintain contact with Zaben by telephone, written correspondence, and third-party intermediaries, such as Halima Zaben.

During one three-way call placed by Halima connecting Lemmons with Zaben, who was then at Fishkill, Zaben gave Lemmons the name and phone number of an American Muslim in Egypt. He was to be one of his primary contacts overseas.[8]

On January 14, 2000, Lemmons completed his parole supervision by the Florida Department of Parole. Without that he would not have been legally able to travel to Saudi Arabia and Egypt. His first trip, in March 2000, was arranged by the president of the Islamic Center of Gainesville, Mohamed Bahmaid. Lemmons returned to Florida in June 2000 and approached Bahmaid, asking for advice in getting involved in jihad overseas. In an interview with the Joint Terrorist Task Force (JTTF), Bahmaid said he tried to discourage Lemmons from going back overseas and encouraged him instead to remain in Florida. Lemmons, however, was not persuaded. He made another trip to Egypt in October 2000 and stayed there, "studying," for eight months. He also married an Egyptian woman whom he met, and they eventually had two sons together.

When he returned to Florida the second time, in June 2001, he met a man at the Islamic Center of Gainesville whose name appears in several JTTF investigation folders in cases involving money laundering and funding of terrorist organizations. According to an informant whom the FBI deemed credible, the man was identified as the local contact for al Qaeda but has not, to this date, been charged with a crime in relation to these cases. He was also associated with another subject of interest to both FBI and JTTF interest, not only for being a possible recruiter of terrorists but also an associate of Abdel Rahman, the Blind Sheikh, convicted in the World Trade Center bombing.

In January 2003, Lemmons moved to the Melbourne, Florida, area and started working for Filter Research Company, which was owned by the man he met in Gainesville in 2001. He also landed a job in a clothing store where he met another individual who, according to intelligence sources, was also under investigation at the time for alleged terrorist-related activity. Investigators observed both Edwin Lemmons and the man from the clothing store regularly meeting with the associate of Abdel Rahman at the mosque in Melbourne.

On April 30, 2003, investigators from Operation Hades listened to a call from inmate Abdel Zaben to an individual in the Bronx, New York, named Cedric Holmes. In the conversation, Zaben exhorted Holmes to be strong in his faith and offered to have him travel to Florida and meet with Lemmons, whom Zaben referred to as Assad. He told Holmes that Assad could assist him in his Islamic education by overseas travel, just as he had done for Assad. Investigators identified Holmes as a former inmate at Fishkill state prison and a convert of Zaben's. Holmes had recently been released on parole supervision and was ineligible for out of state travel or overseas travel without the express written consent of his parole officer. For this reason he did not make the trip.

In the fall of 2002, information was received from a confidential source cultivated by investigators from the Florida JTTF stating that all these suspects were close associates. This informant, whom the JTTF considered reliable, went on to say that Lemmons should be considered a "significant concern" and an extremist with radical Islamic views akin to the Taliban. Lemmons himself confirmed this in a conversation with Zaben, stating, "If someone said I was extreme, I would say OK."[9] Agents from the Florida JTTF set up surveillance on all the subjects mentioned, hoping to gain further information on their activities to determine if in fact any laws had been violated. It was also at this time that Lemmons and another man of Middle Eastern descent started going to a firing range in Melbourne. They were observed shooting AK-47 and SKS assault rifles while practicing combat shooting tactics such as "cover and concealment"—not exactly the usual activities of two guys out for a day at the range.

In conversations recorded by investigators, Lemmons told Zaben that he was planning on moving his entire family to Egypt and finding a job at a friend's factory. In the middle of this conversation Lemmons asked him, "How do you say 'big truck' in Arabic?" Zaben proceeds to tell him and then he repeats, "I have to learn how to say 'big truck.'"[10] This goes on numerous times, causing suspicion among the investigators monitoring the conversations. If Lemmons already spoke fluent Arabic, he would know how to say something as simple as "big truck." What message was he trying to communicate to Zaben? What was the connection between the factory and the "big truck"? What was known: in intelligence circles, the word "factory" was often a euphemism for a bomb-making facility.

Zaben went on to tell Lemmons that he had associates in Saudi Arabia. Lemmons confirmed that he also had friends there. Such an exchange reflects another cryptic method, in this case used to confirm mutual associates in a cause without revealing their names. Lemmons finished the conversation saying that a sheikh from New York came to the mosque in Melbourne and spoke. After the service, the sheikh prayed for Lemmons that Allah would make him a lion against the infidels. Coincidentally, after listening to this conversation, investigators received a Department of Defense bulletin dated June 2003 with a decoded message from an Islamic website that stated, "The attack will occur when Florida hits the heart of the lion."

On August 19, 2003, Lemmons boarded a plane to Egypt with his wife and two children. Investigators then received information that Lemmons would be returning alone to the United States to carry out a mission. Fearing the worst, and not wanting to wait to see what might happen, members of JTTF arrested Edwin Lemmons at the Orlando International Airport for violation of U.S. Code Title 18 section 922-G1, "possession of a firearm by a convicted felon"—a result of the firing-range outing. The arrest took place on September 6, 2003, five days before the anniversary of 9/11.

At that time, the decision to arrest Lemmons was controversial. On one side of the argument were NYPD Intelligence, the CIA, and the

Inspector General's Office, all of which wanted to delay the arrest and keep Lemmons under close surveillance with the hope that he would lead them to other members of his cell. He might also lead them to the location where the weapons or explosives for the planned assault might have been smuggled into the country. The drawback was that this would have required additional time, manpower, and technical resources to follow both Lemmons and his associates in the United States and abroad. The other side of the argument was led by the JTTF in Florida (the New York JTTF Office was strangely detached from the decision-making process), which advocated arresting Lemmons immediately with the hope that, being faced with the full fury of the U.S. government and the threat of prison, he would flip and become a "cooperating individual." In the words of one JTTF-Florida investigator, "He'll spill his guts."

The fierce division between these two camps over how to work this case was nothing new. It had begun back in 2002 when investigators from New York first went to Florida with all the information gathered on Lemmons, Zaben, Egypt, Yemen, and the prison recruitment process. The Florida Department of Law Enforcement and the Gainesville Police Department members assigned to JTTF-Florida had been enthusiastically cooperative with the New York contingent, assisting with logistical support, surveillance, phone records, and background information on the Islamic Center. It was the special agent assigned to JTTF-Florida whose objections to the presence of New York law enforcement officers on his turf that had led to accusations of jurisdictional meddling. The agent went overboard, spouting off about how his office was better equipped to conduct the investigation alone without the interference of investigators from New York. After all, he reasoned, what interest did New York have in any of this?

Detective Sergeant James Murphy from NYPD responded by reminding him that New York had lost almost three thousand people on 9/11 and that was enough of a motivating factor for them to follow any terrorist lead originating in New York to wherever it happened to take them.

While that argument traveled from Florida to New York and then to FBI headquarters in Washington, precious time was being wasted. It became apparent that we had learned very little about working together after 9/11, and once again egos were bruised. In the end, the U.S. Attorney's Office went forward with the Florida JTTF recommendation for immediate arrest.

Once in custody, Lemmons was advised of his rights. Agents went forth with the processing of the arrest and initial questioning. What did Lemmons have to say? Would he provide any information?

Investigators from New York requested permission to at least sit in on the interrogation. FBI response? Denied. The same investigators then requested an opportunity to talk with Lemmons after the initial interrogation by JTTF. They were informed by the special agent in charge that Lemmons had been advised of that fact and that he did not wish to speak with authorities from New York. A standing order was then placed in the county jail where Lemmons was being held that no outside law enforcement officers were permitted to speak with him. Once again, it appeared that nothing was learned about cooperation between agencies.

Shortly thereafter, Lemmons was brought before the court and entered a plea of guilty to the initial charge. After Lemmons had been sentenced, he did speak with NYPD detectives. He told them that he was at no time ever informed that they were outside the room where he was being held and that they had wanted to speak with him. He stated that if asked, he would have agreed to speak with them at the time. It is difficult to determine the veracity of this statement by Lemmons. Perhaps he was simply pitting one side against the other. As a career criminal he was keenly aware of turf wars among law enforcement officers.

The results of the interrogation were not productive. Following the mentoring of his recruiter, Abdel Zaben, Lemmons clammed up and said nothing incriminating. He was a good Muslim brother following Sharia law and would not give information about anyone. When threatened with the possibility of imprisonment, he laughed. How foolish of these infidels to think that he would fear this. He had been in Hades before, and he had not only survived but had thrived. He knew that there were good brothers he would meet, sympathetic clergy, and that he would have access to visitors and phones while he did his time. He knew the limits of the charge on which they had arrested him and that the federal judge was bound by the sentencing guidelines to impose the sentence of twenty-seven months. He also knew that most prosecutors leap at a plea. It's the quickest and easiest way to close a case with a successful prosecution. In exchange for the speedy plea, it was agreed that Lemmons would be allowed to serve his time in Florida where he had family and not to return to New York.

In the eyes of those not intimately familiar with the case, he seemed like just another ex-con back in prison on a gun charge. What, if anything, would he have to do with international terrorism and prison radicalization?

If it were not for the Memorial Institute for the Prevention of Terrorism (MIPT), his connection would have been forgotten. Funded by the Department of Homeland Security, the institute maintains a database on terrorists and their cases since 1968—cases of people like Abdel Rahman, Ramsey Yusef, and El Sayyid Nosair. The history and activities of groups such as Islamic Jihad and al Qaeda also are archived there. Because of this, MIPT knew enough after reviewing the particulars of the case from New York sources to take the case of the United States versus Lemmons and archive it under the post-9/11 terrorism records. It remains there as a classified terrorism case.

It's almost like the closing scene from the movie *Indiana Jones and the Raiders of the Lost Ark*, when you see a sealed wooden crate stamped CLASSIFIED being wheeled into a huge warehouse to be stacked among all the other boxes marked the same. It was stored, and the investigators wiped their hands of it.

Unfortunately it didn't end there. Edwin Lorenzo Lemmons was released from federal custody in May 2006.[11]

CHAPTER 5

With a Little Help from Above

In prison, convicts often pursue religion as a way to help them during their incarceration. It can give them structure, purpose, and hope. Religion can also have a calming effect in such a volatile environment. So important has religion been deemed by society that the New York state legislature included clergy in an official list of persons to whom prisoners could not be denied access. The listed include elected and appointed officials such as the governor, the lieutenant governor, members of the legislature, judges, district attorneys, "and every clergyman or minister, as such terms are defined in section two of the religious corporations law, having charge of a congregation in the county wherein any such facility is situated."[1] Any religious worker could demand to enter a prison in the New York system without restriction.

The original text of the law stated "any minister of the gospel." However, in recognition of the variety of religious organizations in the community today, the wording was amended to include all faiths. That is a powerful authoritarian inroad to a congregation that cannot leave and may be influenced in many ways. NYDOCS officials also have difficulty deciding who is considered a religious worker. Obviously they want to prevent any pseudoclergyman with a shingle on a shack from becoming a religious worker in a facility. Recognizing this, prison administrators have for years sought qualified religious teachers or clergymen to fill the need. As the times have changed, so have the needs. Today, there are as many religions reflected in New York prisons as there are in society at large. Representatives of major religions, such as Christianity, Judaism, Hinduism, Islam, and others as recognized by the U.S. Supreme Court, have a right to tend to the faithful, even if those faithful are in jail. In light of that, civil service positions have been created to fulfill the spiritual needs of inmates. Prison chaplains—priests, pastors, rabbis, monks, nuns, and imams—are an eclectic group, to say the least, but as the investigation of Operation Hades would show, they all have a common thread.

For more than thirty years within the New York State prison system, one man has been responsible for selecting and hiring Islamic clergy for all the facilities: the director of ministerial services. No religious worker, volunteer, or member of an organization seeking contact with any inmates from Sing Sing to Attica can enter a prison without his approval, a policy that seems to be contradictory to what the law said. However, the same law gave prison administrators the authority to establish guidelines by which the law was to be administered. For instance, the commissioner or warden can limit the hours of visitation or issue directives spelling out the process by which a volunteer can participate in a religious program.

First, NYDOCS established a volunteer program, headed by a volunteer coordinator. Then it gave the director of ministerial services oversight of all religious programs, volunteer or otherwise. As a result, tremendous authority and influence was given to the person in the position. Although the commissioner had established a cabinet position of deputy commissioner of programs, that individual often deferred to the expertise of the director of ministerial services in matters relating to religion. When it came to chaplains, particularly Muslim chaplains, the department officials were at a loss in regard to experts. They needed an individual with the backing of an organization to help guide them in the area of Islam. That man was Warith Deen Umar. Umar was the founder and president of the National Association of Muslim Chaplains, the only recognized body that certified Islamic clergy for both the federal and state prison systems at the time. From the time Umar was hired as director of ministerial services, he moved quickly and astutely to establish his position and achieve his goal. As a result, a civil service chaplain could not be hired unless approved by Umar.

Who was this man with so much power and influence in the prison system? Born Wallace Gene Marks in Illinois in 1944, he joined the Nation of Islam movement in the 1960s and became known as Wallace 10X. He quickly came to the attention of the criminal justice system when he and some others, known as the Harlem Five, were arrested in New York City for conspiring to kill NYPD officers. He was convicted of a weapons charge and sentenced to prison, serving his time in New York prisons including Attica and Sing Sing.[2] Following the plot of the familiar prison terrorist story, he pursued a diligent study of Arabic and the Koran, converted to Wahhabi Islam, and changed his name again. After he was released, Umar obtained a certificate of relief from the New York State Board of Parole, a document attesting to his rehabilitation and restoring certain civil privileges. In 1976 he was hired by NYDOCS as one of the first two full-time salaried Muslim chaplains. In 1985 he became director of ministerial services, a position he held until his retirement in 2000. He then served as a volunteer chaplain in New York State and as a paid part-time chaplain for the Federal Bureau of Prisons until 2003. Even after he retired, he continued to exert influence over each of the Islamic clergymen who owed their jobs to him.

Warith Deen Umar's undoing came in February 2003 when he gave an exclusive interview to the *Wall Street Journal* in which he praised the 9/11 hijackers, characterizing them as martyrs.[3] He also went on to describe prison as fertile ground for growing terrorists, arguing that as long as the United States oppresses Muslims, the risk of additional terrorist attacks remains. "Without justice, there will be warfare, and it can come to this country, too," Umar told the reporter, adding that prison "is the perfect recruitment and training grounds for radicalism and the Islamic religion." Not surprisingly, upon release of the interview, he was immediately barred from contact with state and federal inmates.

As a result of this and other investigative factors known to the members of Operation Hades, federal, state, and city law enforcement began a full-scale investigation of all Islamic chaplains in the New York State prison system in the spring of 2003. Prior to the article, investigators only focused on specific chaplains who had associations with Abdel Zaben. This expanded investigation, approved at the highest level of government and continuing at least until 2005, included surveillance, phone data collection, and other techniques to uncover both foreign and domestic radical Islamic influence in the prison system. NYDOCS officials denied that Muslim clergy were being singled out for investigation, but they were.[4] Following findings from Operation Hades, Islamic chaplains were indeed suspect, as federal and state security agencies acknowledged the threat of radical Islamic recruitment, stating that "inmate chapels remain vulnerable to infiltration by religious extremists."[5] A classified addendum to this report detailed cases in which counterterrorism officials asserted that people leading prison prayer sessions—including authorized chaplains, volunteers, and inmates—may have had ties to terrorist groups.[6]

It was true that the reach of some of the men and women chosen to work in the service of Islam within the New York's prison walls extended far beyond them. Some had nefarious criminal backgrounds including murder and extortion. Others had dubious immigration status and ties to Saudi Arabia, Yemen, and Sudan. Yet all of them were chosen by this man, Warith Deen Umar. Many of the imams hired by Umar received sponsorship in the form of financial stipends from foreign governments to travel to Saudi Arabia and other places. Chaplains working for the prison system come into day-to-day contact with inmates. Their offices are "down back"—that is, beyond the administration buildings, where inmates work, eat, and sleep. There is no hiding there. Inmates see you and they talk to you. Chaplains were not isolated from the population as some employees sought to be. Those who did were called derogatorily "palace guards." It would not be thought unusual to see inmates talking to or working for the chaplain.

What investigators found that *was* unusual was the number of high-security inmates who interacted with the Muslim chaplains. For example, several of the clergy had direct contact with such known Islamic terrorists as El Sayyid Nosair, Rashid Baz, and Abdel Nasser Zaben.[7] These inmates worked in the chaplain's office, assisting him in the administration of his duties. One of these was establishing or reestablishing the family bonds of the inmates in their congregation. It was how they did this that caught the attention of the investigators assigned to Operation Hades.

Chaplains have the right and responsibility, under NYDOCS policy directives, to call an inmate's family in the course of their normal duties. For example, if an inmate is injured or hospitalized, a chaplain may call the family. If there is a death in the inmate's family, the chaplain can make the call for the inmate and allow him to talk to his family as part of the bereavement process. When investigators reviewed the phone records from those chaplains, however, they found some oddities about the calls to relatives and associates of the suspected terrorists. First, the chaplains never made the required written record of the calls they placed on behalf of the inmates. The same policy that allowed chaplains to place unrestricted and unmonitored calls for any inmate also stated that a written memo be placed in the inmate's folder stating who received the call and the reason that the call was necessary. Second, there was an unusually high volume of calls made—in the thousands—to known radical Islamic organizations and associates of incarcerated terrorists in the United States, the Middle East, and North Africa.[8] Last, there was a procedure in place for the inmate to reimburse the prison for the cost of the call. This was not done either.

What investigators did find was that the inmate or his significant other would often purchase calling cards and utilize them through the chaplain's phone, placing calls out of state or overseas. Such was the case for Abdel and Halima Zaben. Theirs was not a novel security breach by a radical Islamic inmate working in a chaplain's office. One of the plotters of the first World Trade Center attack was an inmate in Attica—El Sayyid Nosair—who had unfettered access to the phone in the Islamic chaplain's office by reason of his program assignment as the chaplain's clerk.

The investigators in Operation Hades also examined the relationships among religious volunteers, guest speakers, and visiting clergy. At one point investigators discovered that an official from the Council on American-Islamic Relations (CAIR) headquarters in Washington, D.C., visited Fishkill Correctional Facility while Zaben was there. Members of Hades were also examining the use of inmate charitable donations and fundraising for pseudo-Islamic charities with possible ties to terrorists or terrorist organizations. Investigators had come to believe that a radical Islamic recruitment cell was operating in the prison system, and they wanted to determine if the clergy played any role in helping the cell, either knowingly or not.[9] Ignorance by employees when it comes to dealing with inmates on a daily basis was something that the department strove to remove through training. Chaplains were no exception to the dangerous pitfalls of being conned.

In the normal prison setting, inmates visit a chaplain because he cares, is understanding, and is willing to help by listening and providing counsel. Some inmates, however, visit a chaplain because he has a soft touch. They know they may be able to put a move on him and get what they want—a free phone call or letter sent out. As innocuous as these two things sound, overseeing communication is critical to maintaining a safe and secure environment in a correctional facility. All calls that an inmate makes in prison are subject to monitoring—for good reason. In the past, inmates have used the telephones to plot escapes, sell narcotics, or order contract murders. Written correspondence is also closely scrutinized to see if contraband or hidden messages are being smuggled in or out of the prison. The U.S. courts have acknowledged in several landmark cases the necessity of such strict security controls.[10] Inmates, of course, are always looking for a way around them.

In their book *Games Criminals Play*, Bud Allen and Diana Bosta outline the progression that inmates use to test the resolve of prison employees.[11] First, a prisoner asks a chaplain, for example, to take out a letter to a loved one because he can't afford a stamp. Then he asks the chaplain to meet that loved one to pick up a package because the inmate's relative can't afford to travel up to the prison to visit the inmate. The inmate reels him in, and next thing you know, the chaplain is bringing packages in on a regular basis. What the prison employee doesn't consider until it's too late is what could be in the package—drugs, a handcuff key, a gun, or any other kind of contraband. There's a reason this practice is called being "conned."

Hundreds of case files in New York alone detail this scenario, in which prison clergymen from all religions have been apprehended, arrested, and convicted for promoting prison contraband, bribe receiving, or official misconduct.[12] To be sure, not all inmates who go to speak with the chaplain are looking for something other than spiritual guidance, and not all chaplains are so easily duped by disingenuous converts. The vast majority of religious workers in correctional facilities are sincere, dedicated individuals whose concern for their flock is unquestioned. However, it only takes one or two to create a security threat that can go beyond the prison walls. In Zaben's case, it took several.

Salahuddin Muhammad, aka Leon Lawson, Leon Ross, Shanhan Allah, or Shanhan Lawson, was born in New York City in March 1951. In addition to being a prison imam, he is also the spiritual leader of the Masjid Al Jihad al Akbar (renamed Masjid Al Ikhlas in 2003) in Newburgh, New York. He is an adjunct professor at Marist College and Mercy College and a listed member of the Islamic Correctional Foundation of America. He has also been arrested twelve times for charges of robbery, assault, criminal possession of a weapon, and grand larceny. He has five violent felony convictions and spent more than twelve years in a state prison, after which he has made the haj to

Mecca with the financing of the Saudi Arabian government. He was a close friend and associate of Warith Deen Umar, who recommended to the deputy commissioner of programs in 2000 that he replace Umar as the director of ministerial services after his retirement.[13]

While he was employed in Fishkill state prison, Muhammad had Zaben assigned to his office as chaplain's clerk. Zaben held that position for more than five years, during which time the imam allowed him unfettered access to the office phone. Many of Zaben's calls were to countries in the Middle East and North Africa. Others were to Texas, Virginia, Florida, and New York City. Zaben was also allowed to receive calls on the phone in the office. Operation Hades recorded several conversations between Zaben and people in the Middle East in which he gave them the phone number of the facility, the imam's extension, and specific times to call. He also told them they shouldn't worry if he is not in the office when the call comes in, that "Imam Salahuddin is a good brother. He will come and get me." He went on to say that the chaplain would act as his personal secretary in putting the calls through to him.[14]

Investigators looked into whether Muhammad was being duped by Zaben or if he were a knowing, willing participant. The answer was found in the NYDOCS data system and the chaplain's personnel history. Several years prior to meeting Zaben, Muhammad had been formally disciplined and a letter placed in his folder for providing a Muslim inmate unlimited access to his office phone. At the time of that incident, the department simply transferred the inmate to another prison and placed a "flag" on his separation comments that he was never again to be housed in the same facility where Salahuddin Muhammad was employed. No changes were made to the office phone. No restrictions on incoming or outgoing calls were placed on the chaplain. But it is clear from the counseling memorandums given to him as a result of the incident that such liberties were not allowed.

Since Muhammad's office phone was not subject to monitoring or recording under the guidelines that existed then, the members of Operation Hades went to the Manhattan District Attorney's Office early in 2003 to request that Assistant District Attorney Dan McGulicuddy be assigned to the investigation. McGulicuddy was instrumental in obtaining court authorization to install a pen register on the chaplain's phone.[15] A pen register is an electronic device that records the numbers dialed from a phone. This was the first-known court order issued under the Terrorist Intercept Act in New York. Installing such a wire was not easy, especially in a prison. The phone lines were located inside a secure area and the only access was through an employee. So, to maintain the confidentiality of the investigation, an individual from the technical support unit of the Manhattan District Attorney's Office was disguised as a phone repairman to enter the facility under the pretense of responding to a malfunction complaint. He was granted access to the room, and while the escort officer was not looking, he slipped the device onto the line dedicated to the chaplain's office. Once it was in place, the information from that phone flowed to the team of investigators assigned to Operation Hades. The data collected provided details on the origination and destination of all calls made from Muhammad's phone. This information, along with other data and surveillance, was used to help identify individuals in New York City and abroad who were involved in the recruitment cell. The foreign phone numbers identified were forwarded to the National Security Agency.

Not only did Muhammad knowingly offer his phone line, but he also personally spoke with and met two of Zaben's New York City associates, Basman Aziz and Hatem Mussalem. Both Aziz and Mussalem were Palestinians with Jordanian citizenship and passports who had visited Zaben in prison on numerous occasions. Mussalem lived on Albemarle Road in the Prospect Park section of Brooklyn. He was three years older than Zaben and had an electrical contracting business. He had no criminal history in the United States. Aziz was two years younger than Zaben and owned two furniture stores in the Bay Ridge section of Brooklyn. He was the individual previously mentioned who owned the house at 246 74th Street in Brooklyn, across the street from El Sayyid Nosair's associates. When Mussalem arrived in the United States, he gave his address as 554 Atlantic Avenue in Brooklyn. That is the address of the Al Farooq mosque, which El Sayyid Nosair attended along with Abdel Rahman, the Egyptian cleric known as the Blind Sheikh. The location was known to authorities as far back as the late 1980s as a hotbed of radical Islamic teaching that provided funds to Osama bin Laden and the other *mujahideen* in Afghanistan. The funding was provided through donations to the Al-Kifah Refugee Fund.[16]

The connection between Abdel Zaben's associates and the individuals involved in the first attack on the World Trade Center was too coincidental for investigators from Operation Hades to overlook. On several occasions, conversations between Zaben and these two men were recorded. Listening to them talk convinced investigators of deep-rooted anti-Semitism and a commitment to the cause of Islamic terrorism. Twice they were heard discussing incidents in the Middle East that had resulted in deaths. Although they were not directly involved in those incidents, the conversations demonstrated their ability to acquire specific information from outside or overseas sources—the exact body count and real-time details of a terrorist attack—that was not publicly available at the time. It also revealed their hatred for nonbelievers.[17]

In one of the incidents discussed, two men had been killed on Kafan Street in Ramallah on the West Bank in front of a school. Zaben asked Aziz if the morale of the *mujahideen* was high, and Aziz said it was. Another time, Zaben innocently asked Aziz how everything was going. Aziz responded, "Two killed, four injured." Zaben then asks, "Us?" and Aziz responds, "No, the pigs." Zaben is noticeably happy and asks where the *mujahideen* came from, to which Aziz says, "From Nablus, which is near us." They go on to discuss Zaben's possible release from prison and agree that if and when it does happen, they will go to the Middle East together and "do business."[18]

Members of Operation Hades also conducted surveillance of Aziz and Mussalem and saw them entering several mosques that were of interest to counterterrorism experts. One was the mosque in Brooklyn frequented by Rashid Baz and known as the Islamic Society of Bay Ridge. The other location was the Masjid Dar-Da'awa in Queens, a mosque that was owned by the Islamic Service Foundation of Richardson, Texas.[19] Both Mussalem and Basman Aziz had been directed by inmate Zaben to forward any messages through Muhammad's office. On one occasion Zaben went as far as to give the phone number and the extension of the Fishkill state prison chaplain's office to Mussalem. Zaben also instructed newly released inmates whom he had recruited to contact Mussalem for assistance.

This use of the clergy by Zaben's associates was phenomenal. At one point, investigators from Operation Hades were looking at more than seven thousand phone calls from the chaplain's office while Zaben was the clerk.[20] Zaben's ability to bend another Muslim's will to his was not limited to the manipulation of the chaplain's phone privileges. In addition to providing a telephone service for Zaben,

Muhammad actually went to the store in Brooklyn owned by Basman Aziz, following Zaben's direction. While there, Muhammad made arrangements to use facility funds to purchase several Persian rugs from Aziz's store and have them delivered to the prison. He didn't need FedEx or UPS—he had Zaben's friends to make the drop. Aziz and Mussalem entered the facility with a marked van and delivered the rugs. At the chaplain's insistence, neither the van nor the occupants were searched for contraband or weapons by the guards at the prison gate. Some investigators believed that Muhammad received a financial benefit from the purchase and delivery of these items to Zaben in the prison, obviously a huge violation of the NYDOCS's policy for procurement of items with government funds. As investigators studied the paper trail of this transaction, they found that two officials, the deputy superintendent and the steward, had signed off on the purchase. When the warden of the prison was questioned by the author regarding this incident, he admitted that egregious mistakes were made and internal controls had not been followed.[21]

At other times, also at Zaben's direction, Muhammad solicited donations from inmates for several charities, among them the Holy Land Foundation, Help the Needy, and his own mosque in Newburgh. As noted, the first two charities have been identified by the State Department and the U.S. Attorney General's Office as using their funds to support terrorism. Upon freezing the American assets of the Holy Land Foundation, President George W. Bush described the fact that they had raised $13 million from U.S. residents to fund Hamas efforts to "indoctrinate children to grow up into suicide bombers" and "recruit suicide bombers and to support their families."[22] The Holy Land Foundation was forwarding funds raised to Hamas, to which Zaben belonged. Help the Needy was alleged to be funneling its donations to Iraq in violation of U.S. sanctions.

One of the men arrested and convicted for collecting and distributing funds for Help the Needy was a New York state prison chaplain, Osama Alwahaidy. Alwahaidy was the imam at Auburn Correctional Facility where Zaben had spent four years. At the time of Alwahaidy's arrest, his inmate clerk was Rashid Baz, the Brooklyn Bridge Shooter—a convicted Islamic terrorist, Hamas sympathizer, and close associate of Zaben. In their zeal to arrest Alwahaidy and issue an immediate press release, federal authorities completely overlooked the connection between him and the radical Islamic inmates in the prison system.

Members of Operation Hades were not consulted by the U.S. attorney's office or the FBI for information they had that would connect the financing with the recruitment of inmates by radical Islamic organizations. Territorial rights and personal egos apparently caused the oversight.

The third charity, the Masjid Al Jihad al Akbar (and later Masjid Al Ikhlas), was simply a way for Muhammad to receive money from inmates. In street terms, it was a kickback, at the very least an administrative violation of the NYDOCS employees' rules. The NYDOCS manual, which he was issued, informs all employees that they are specifically prohibited from accepting gifts or gratuities in any form from an inmate without the approval of the commissioner or superintendent.[23] The manual goes on to warn that doing so may be construed as violating section 73 of the New York State Public Officers Law.[24] This was not the first time he had crossed the line while a chaplain. In 1995 he was cited for "an improper relationship and dealings with an inmate." The inmate, Abdul Salahuddin (no relation) was serving a life sentence for murder and manslaughter when he was hired by the chaplain to be his clerk. Again, one of his privileges as clerk was access to the chaplain's phone. Following the administrative ruling, the inmate was transferred to another facility and the incident was noted in Muhammad's personnel folder. After it was reviewed by a sympathetic Warith Deen Umar in the central office, no further disciplinary action or investigation was taken.

This same chaplain had another clerk who was of interest to counterterrorism investigators. Arrested in 1990, Abdullah Nagi was serving a sentence of seven to twenty-one years for manslaughter in the first degree. Of Yemeni extraction, Nagi was living in the Buffalo area at the time of his arrest. When investigators from Operation Hades examined his prison documents they found, through phone and visitor records, that he had direct ties to the "Lackawanna Six." Although he was associated with several of the members, he himself was in prison at the time of their arrest and was not named in the indictment. The Lackawanna Six was a group of young Yemeni Americans living in the Buffalo area who had attended a jihad training camp in Afghanistan in the spring of 2001.[25] This, to investigators, was another example of the connection between radical Islamic influences in the outside world with those in prison. It was at this time that officials working with investigators in Operation Hades became concerned about Zaben's influence not only with the chaplain at Fishkill but also with the entire Muslim inmate population in the prison.

In November 2003, Zaben appeared before the parole board for his initial hearing to determine if he should be released. In rendering its decision, the board denied his release based on a confidential memorandum submitted by the Intelligence Division that outlined the preliminary findings of Operation Hades and stated that "the assigned investigators feel that Abdel Nasser Zaben presents a grave risk to the national security both here and overseas."[26] This decision led to another reclassification of Zaben's security level (he was restricted from being moved anywhere without the written consent of the Intelligence Division). While the reclassification probably alerted him to the fact that he was being watched, it also was meant to unnerve him, perhaps causing him to slip up and inadvertently provide useful information. Subsequently, he was transferred from the Fishkill medium-security prison to the maximum-security Shawangunk Correctional Facility in Ulster County, a move that was often normal procedure following a parole rejection.

Salahuddin Muhammad came to national attention in May 2009 when he was interviewed by the *New York Times* immediately after the arrest of four former inmates for plotting to blow up synagogues and shoot down military aircraft in New York with Stinger missiles. The ex-cons at the time were attending his mosque in Newburgh as part of a prison release/reintegration program. He told reporters he had never known or heard of any Islamic jihadists in his prison ministry. According to the *New York Times*,

> Mr. Muhammad said his years' working with Muslims in prison has turned up little actual evidence that many or any become radicalized behind bars. "I don't hear any of that wild stuff," he said, "and if I did hear it, I would stomp it out. It's totally un-Islamic."[27]

He seemed to have forgotten his own clerks.

Even with a move to a more secure environment, it did not take Zaben long to become intimately acquainted with the Islamic chaplain there, Cyril Rashid. Also known as Cyril Clark, Rashid had seven prior arrests and three felony convictions with charges of robbery, criminal possession of a weapon, assault, and aggravated harassment. He was hired by NYDOCS at the direction of Warith Deen Umar in 1986. He then became a member of the Salafi Society of North America. Rashid had been assigned to several New York prisons prior to his request to work in Shawangunk. Rashid, like all the other imams in the prison system, handpicked his own inmate clerk.

Rashid's clerk prior to Zaben's arrival was Yassir Ahmed. A native of Saudi Arabia with ties to Yemen, Ahmed was serving a sentence of twenty-five years to life for murder. Ahmed had participated in the prison's secretive Talem Circle meetings. The group's objective at Shawangunk state prison was to forge an alliance between Middle Eastern and U.S.-born inmates to work together in the jihad.[28]

Confidential sources placed near Zaben in Shawangunk revealed that he was again exercising control over the Muslim prison community, including Chaplain Rashid. With that information, the investigators of Operation Hades initiated blanketed surveillance of Rashid, including telephone record interception and installing a GPS device on his vehicle. It was during that time that Detective Dave Miller, assigned to the operation, noted that the pen register data from the chaplain's office in Fishkill showed a call placed from the prison to a Muslim-owned business in Liberty, a town in New York's Catskill Mountains. An investigator from the New York State Police assigned to Operation Hades found that Cyril Rashid also had an address in Liberty. The business, known as Sweet Sunnah, was owned by Abdel Aziz Benadim. Sweet Sunnah is a retail company that sells personal care products and nutritional supplements. While doing a background investigation on him, Senior Investigator Ken Torreggiani from the Inspector General's Office uncovered that Benadim was a former NYDOCS chaplain who had been fired for unauthorized dealings with inmates in the Sullivan Correctional Facility in the town of Fallsburg.

Valuable information continued to come into the operation regarding the relationship among these three chaplains: Salahuddin Muhammad, Cyril Rashid, and Abdel Aziz Benadim. The chief of the Liberty police department reported receiving information in October 2003 that both Rashid and Benadim had recently traveled to Egypt, Saudi Arabia, and Morocco. He went on to tell of unrest in the Liberty mosque, attended by Rashid and Benadim, caused by the preaching of radical beliefs.

Based on this and other information, Assistant DA McGulicuddy requested and received the telephone records of eleven phone numbers in Liberty associated with Rashid and Benadim. The toll records showed calls to the United Kingdom, Spain, the United Arab Emirates, Australia, Morocco, Germany, Canada, Bermuda, and South Africa as well as four calls to a gun store in Connecticut owned by Abdus Sabur Muhammad. Clearly the clergy had more than heaven on their mind.

Still, at that time investigators did not have a solid connection between these clergyman and inmate Zaben until Torreggiani found a "kited" letter from Zaben to an inmate in another prison named Zayd Rashid. A native of Guyana, Rashid was serving a sentence of twenty years to life for a brutal robbery homicide committed in New York City in 1982. The terms "kite" and "kited letter" are prison jargon for a written communication from or to a prisoner that bypasses the normal correspondence procedure. More often than not it contains a concealed message. The methodology for sending such communiqués is limited only by the inmate's imagination.

The interesting thing about the kited letter from Zaben was not the letter itself, but the individual who delivered it, former chaplain Abdel Aziz Benadim. Even though he had been fired by NYDOCS for misconduct, he was still permitted to visit New York prisons as a spiritual counselor. With this access, he was the perfect courier for confidential messages. This was another example of the breakdown between the Security Department of NYDOCS and the Volunteer Program Department. It was embarrassing for NYDOCS officials to try to explain it to the other law enforcement officials working under the umbrella of Operation Hades.

Investigators also found that Benadim was the imam and Rashid was the secretary-treasurer of the Liberty mosque. They began looking very closely at the mosque and its surrounding area.

The Catskills region has had a long history of vacation homes and resorts used by New York City residents since the 1920s. In the 1980s, the area fell on hard economic times, and many of the resorts and bungalow colonies closed. The general makeup of the population changed, and new arrivals of different religious faiths established places of worship, such as ashrams and Islamic centers. Several other individuals new to the area who were attending the mosque in Liberty drew the interest of the Operation Hades team.

In the fall of 2003, Bilal Abdul Haqq, listed as the mosque's security officer, had a verbal confrontation with an official at the local hospital. During the argument, he accused the Israeli government of committing the attacks on September 11. Another recent Liberty resident, Ronald Ali, also known as Ronald Philips, had a commercial pilot license and according to FBI Automated Case Support reports, he had worked for a Department of Defense contractor and held a top-secret security clearance prior to being fired by his employer, ENSCO, Inc. The report stated that following the U.S. invasion of Afghanistan, Ali told the company that he could "not support the military industrial complex and the effort to destroy Islam."[29] ENSCO officials told federal agents that although he had top-secret clearance, he was not working on any secret projects at the time. Investigators subpoenaed his employment records and found that Ali was a retired U.S. Navy aircraft weapons technician who had worked on weapons systems for various aircraft including the F-4, F-14, and A-10. In December 2002, Ali traveled to Frankfurt, Germany, returning later that month. In March 2003, Ali again flew to Frankfurt. Frankfurt is home to a sizable number of Muslim organizations, including the Islamische Gemeinschaft in Deutschland, an organization of Arab Muslims close to the Muslim Brotherhood of Egypt, in which such modern-day jihadists as Ayman al-Zawahiri, for a long time the second-in-command of al Qaeda, have established their roots.

Ali, today believed to be in Yemen, was not the only member of the Liberty mosque in Germany at the time. Mustafa Abu Abdullah, or Lawrence Holst, a former member of the U.S. military, had emigrated to Germany and obtained citizenship. He communicated with the mosque's leadership in December 2003 via cell phone from overseas. The Special Investigative Unit report on the mosque went on to say that other individuals in the area of Benadim's mosque had suspicious activity in their backgrounds and shared Abdullah's radical views, warranting further investigation.[30]

Shortly thereafter letters written by two inmates intended for Cyril Rashid were intercepted. In the letters, one from an African American Muslim inmate and the other from a foreign-born Muslim inmate, the inmates spoke of Rashid's desire to go to Yemen and teach English in the "camps." The author of one of the letters, Yassir Ahmed, had been Rashid's clerk. In that letter, Ahmed provided Rashid with names and phone numbers of contacts in Saudi Arabia and Yemen who would assist him when he arrived. The "camps" referred to were training camps for foreign-born recruits who needed to learn English in order to assimilate into American society. These names, addresses, and phone numbers were forwarded to members of the CIA working with Operation Hades.

One of the biggest problems in the prison clergy hiring system was the background checks of potential clergy, particularly Islamic clergy. In the past, the certifying body for Muslims was the National Association of Muslim Chaplains. In 2003 investigators found that the organization had been founded by Warith Deen Umar and was using his home address as its home base. After his interview with the *Wall Street Journal* and his subsequent banishment from all contact with state and federal prisons, a void in the certification process existed. There arose another certifying body for Muslim clergy—the Majalis-Ashura of Metropolitan New York.

The president of the Majalis-Ashura was Al-Amin Abdul-Latif. Like Warith Deen Umar before him, Abdul-Latif was a former inmate who had converted to Islam while in prison. Upon his release, he too was hired as a chaplain for NYDOCS. His sponsor for the job was Warith Deen Umar.

Members of Majalis-Ashura used two addresses of record when sending official documents to NYDOCS personnel requesting information on potential chaplains. One was 1221 Atlantic Avenue in Brooklyn, a boarded-up storefront around the corner from the Al Taqwa mosque. The other was 122 South 25th Street in Wyandanch, which was Abdul-Latif's house.

One of the chaplains certified by the majalis was Abubakr Abdul-Latif, Al-Amin's son. The family connection continued when Abubakr's prior employment reference turned out to be his mother, Al-Amin's former wife. This was overlooked by the new director of ministerial services, Rahim Ismail, who worked in New York but lived in Tobyhanna, Pennsylvania, the same town that had hosted a jihad camp for young Muslims in August 2004.[31] One of the keynote speakers at the jihad camp happened to be Al-Amin Abdul-Latif. Around this same time investigators received information from the Joint Terrorist Task Force that Abdul-Latif was a subject of interest in an ongoing investigation along with several other members of the *majalis*.[32] Thus another certifying body was invalidated. Faced with no independent ecclesiastical body for certifying Muslim chaplains, the commissioner ordered that every potential Muslim chaplain be investigated by the Inspector General's Office and members of Operation Hades.

Islamic chaplains were not the only weak link in the prison security system. In 2003 at Attica Correctional Facility, a Catholic nun acting as a spiritual adviser to an inmate was caught allowing him to make unauthorized calls. The inmate was David Gilbert, the convicted domestic terrorist. The nun thought she was assisting Gilbert in placing calls to his son, but she was actually helping him contact a noted Palestinian Rights activist living in New York City. The activist often entertained individuals from a wide spectrum of political, educational, and ethnic backgrounds. Among the people who he had hosted in his home were convicted domestic terrorists and Iraqi nationals—interesting houseguests considering that several meetings were just prior to the Republican National Convention in New York and immediately after the U.S. invasion of Iraq.[33]

Gilbert was transferred to Clinton Correctional Facility, and the nun was cited administratively. No further action was taken by the Attica prison officials.[34] This was just another example of clergy members assisting terrorists, giving them a little help from above.

CHAPTER 6

Paying Attention to the Past

What relationship, if any, do past domestic terrorist acts have with the current threat of homegrown terrorism or any future minatory radicalization? I believe there are lessons to be learned from past events that could prevent the repetition of violence. Just a generation ago both the United States and Europe were exposed to a wave of anarchy and vehemence from ideologues who were committed to revolutionary change by any means necessary.

In 1969, the same year Abdel Zaben was born, an event important to the study of counterterrorism occurred in Port Huron, Michigan, during the height of the anti–Vietnam War movement in the United States. In that year, a radical domestic terrorist group was formed after infighting within the ranks of a nonviolent protest group escalated, causing it to fragment. This group, Students for a Democratic Society (SDS), was formed in 1960 at the University of Michigan at Ann Arbor. Two years later, it held a national convention in Port Huron and issued its treatise on social change. The SDS expressed a desire to use civil disobedience and other nonviolent means to cause change with social, political, and economic policy within the government.[1]

After several years of nonviolent protest, a segment within that group became disillusioned with the results and wanted to take action—violent action—against the U.S. government. These members called themselves the Weathermen, after a line in a Bob Dylan song, "You don't need a weatherman to know which way the wind blows."[2] The first mention of this new group appears in the June 1969 issue of the

SDS newsletter.[3] That same year this group of extremists declared war on the U.S. government, announcing it would "attack a symbol of American injustice."[4] It titled its first campaign, a series of violent acts that took place in Chicago in October 1969, the Days of Rage.

Chicago had already experienced a sampling of what was to occur. One year prior, during the Democratic Convention, anti-war demonstrators had clashed violently with members of the Chicago Police Department. As a result, several leaders of the protest group were indicted by an Illinois grand jury, and their trial commenced in September 1969. It was during that proceeding, and with an enormous media presence assigned to cover what was considered by some a circus act, that the Weathermen began their four-day siege. First there was a rally in Lincoln Park on October 8, a gathering for which the city had refused to issue a permit. Then the group ran through the streets smashing windows of cars, buildings, and stores, and committing other acts of violence. Police officers called to the scene were attacked. When the riot ended, the cost to the city was hundreds of thousands of dollars in damage, overtime, and medical costs.

The group next moved on both geographically and to a more destructive methodology, which included explosives. On March 6, 1970, just before noon, an explosion erupted in an elegant brownstone building in New York City's historic Greenwich Village neighborhood. The building's owner was James P. Wilkerson. In it was his daughter, Cathy Wilkerson, a member of the Weathermen who was out on bail after assaulting a police officer during the Chicago demonstrations. Wilkerson and her friend Kathy Boudin, also a member of the group, survived the blast. Three other members were not so lucky. When police searched the remains of the building, they discovered dynamite, artillery shells, and pipe bombs.[5] The Weathermen were using the home as a bomb factory. Both Wilkerson and Boudin fled the scene, and the group changed its name to the Weather Underground.

This setback did not stop the group from continuing its violent anarchist mission. In fact, for the next twelve years the members of the Weather Underground continued with bombings while moving about from safe house to safe house around the United States as they were pursued by federal, state, and local law enforcement.

The Weather Underground was not the only revolutionary or subversive group being investigated by law enforcement officials at this time. Nor was the violence limited to the United States. Europe also experienced a rash of domestic terrorism. And it was at this time that the Weather Underground forged alliances with some of the international terrorist groups, including the Red Brigades in Italy and the Baader-Meinhof gang in Germany. The Weather Underground was also linked by the FBI to another domestic terrorist group, the Black Liberation Army (BLA), which had grown out of the Black Panther Party in Oakland.[6] Several BLA members were already serving time in state prisons for the deaths of as many as ten police officers around the country.[7] BLA members had gained a reputation for being ready to shoot on sight any law enforcement officer who crossed their paths. No demonstration, no talk, just bang. They believed what Mao had said, that "power grows out of the barrel of a gun." While not all the groups were aligned philosophically or culturally, the ancient Arab proverb provided the impetus for alliances: "The enemy of my enemy is my friend."

Assistance is necessary for the successful execution of any planned act of terrorism, but the need can make strange bedfellows. There are those who have strongly endorsed the theory that members of the PLO Black September Group who killed eleven Israeli athletes during the Olympics in Munich in 1972 were assisted both financially and with logistical support, such as safe house and transportation, by known European domestic terrorists.[8] Identifying the associations, or "connecting the dots," is vital for any effective counterterrorism program. Often, capturing one member or group can have a domino effect.

Both the Weather Underground and the Black Liberation Army were dealt a serious blow in 1981 by law enforcement with the arrest of the groups' key members for a botched armed robbery in Nyack, New York. Following a lengthy trial, members of the two groups were convicted and sentenced to long prison terms. Some ended up in the custody of the Federal Bureau of Prisons, while many were placed with NYDOCS.

As time moved on, in American society at large many of the issues of the 1960s and '70s also moved on and were forgotten. One of the effects of this societal change was that the radical American domestic terrorists of this period no longer received the attention they had previously. That remained true until Zaben met some of them while at Auburn state prison: the anarchists met the jihadists. The circumstances in which he met these former '60s radicals is intriguing and could not have been accomplished without the help of another inmate from the Middle East, Yousef Saleh, the Deli Bomber.

Saleh was born in Palestine in 1953. His family originated in Ramallah on the West Bank. He was granted Jordanian citizenship and a passport for his travel to the United States. Saleh spent about a year in the Bronx House of Detention during his legal proceedings, and then he was turned over to NYDOCS on April 9, 1980, to begin serving his sentence at Attica. The Inspector General's Office designated him a central monitoring case. This meant that his every movement during his term of imprisonment was to be closely monitored. As investigators would later learn, it was not. After more than two years in Attica, the prison administrators there wanted him removed for "unsuitable behavior," a polite way of saying he was a troublemaker or instigator. He was too "bad" for Attica, which is saying something. Saleh was packed up and sent to Clinton Correctional Facility in Dannemora. In July 1983, he was again transferred, this time for program purposes, to the Great Meadow Correctional Facility near Lake George. While at Great Meadow, he was involved in a riot in which one inmate was killed and numerous others injured. When calm was restored, corrections officials transferred all of the individuals involved. That was how he came to be at Auburn.

Saleh spent thirteen of the next fourteen years at Auburn, where he had the opportunity to meet an eclectic group of convicts that included members of the Black Liberation Army. Although considered by some to be a black nationalist–Marxist organization, the vast majority of the BLA members who were incarcerated in New York State had declared their religion as Islam upon reception into NYDOCS custody, and they regularly attended Jummah services in the facility mosque. It was there that Saleh met many of them and openly discussed the Sunni/Wahabbi view of the Koran, espousing the doctrine of Abdallah Azzam who believed that Islam went beyond any nationalist movement. Saleh also spoke and read Arabic, which all the members of the prison Muslim congregation were encouraged to learn.

Saleh was beginning to lay the groundwork for Zaben. Perhaps prison administrators had misjudged his intelligence. His educational records stated that he had never gone beyond the sixth grade; yet while his dominant language was Arabic, he had a college reading comprehension level in tests taken in English. He was no dummy. He also successfully completed a one-year drafting and design course while incarcerated. It is extremely odd that prison officials allowed a convicted arsonist to attend drafting school. Perhaps they did not consider that the next time Saleh decided to destroy a building, they would be responsible for having taught him where to strategically place the explosives for maximum effect. Trying to explain that to the other law enforcement agents in Operation Hades was another embarrassment for NYDOCS officials.

Just off the transfer bus and waiting in the reception area of the prison, Zaben undoubtedly had heard that he was not the only Palestinian in the Joint and that the other Palestinian inmate was also a Muslim. In every prison reception area are inmates who work as porters and clerks. By virtue of their relationship with the officer in charge of that area, often they can gain access to the incoming and outgoing transfer list days before the buses arrive. They then pass that information along to other inmates for a price. With this information, an inmate can arrange a cell assignment, an arrival party, or even a hit before the new inmate steps off the bus. One analogy would be letting the janitor of JFK airport have access to all the flight manifests. During his orientation, Zaben was informed where and when Muslim services were held and how to request visitation to the mosque. He must have been overjoyed when he finally met Saleh there. Here was someone from his homeland who spoke Arabic and was a devout Muslim. Saleh was also sixteen years older than Zaben, whom Zaben could look up to as a big-brother figure.

Shortly after he entered Auburn, Saleh began working in the prison industry program making license plates. As much of a cliché as that seems, it's not like the movies. Making license plates today involves highly technical work. The New York prison manufacturing program, known as Corcraft Industries, is a lucrative business—both for the state and for the inmates—and license plates are just one of the products produced. The state makes millions while the inmates who work in Industry earn more money than other inmates in menial prison jobs. A convict doing a long bid and who doesn't have the financial resources of family or friends to support him can make license plates, which is the most desired job in the Joint.

Saleh made plates for quite some time until he was slightly injured in an accident in the shop, for which he filed a lawsuit against NYDOCS. New York State ended up paying him a hefty financial settlement.

Members of Operation Hades conducted a review of Saleh's financial transactions during his time in prison, which revealed that the money he received from the settlement and other monies he had earned or received had made its way to the Middle East. They believed that at least some of the funds found their way into the hands of Hamas in Ramallah via a postal box in Panama. It's possible that among the things he learned from former domestic radicals was how to move money overseas and the use of nontraceable P.O. boxes.

While in Auburn prison, Saleh also learned how to move about the prison. It was a skill that he would pass on to Zaben, because at times it was necessary to communicate with other inmates. Although prisons are constructed of concrete and steel to prevent escapes and isolate living quarters, the prison setting offers a variety of means to see other inmates if you're jail-wise. All movement of inmates both outside and within the prison walls is tightly controlled. Still, there are ways to move about in the prison environment more than you might expect.

Convicts go to great lengths to learn of the different ways to meet other convicts.

Inmates start with common events where they can go and consociate. Inmates do not just sit in their cells. They meet in the mess hall, in the prison auditorium where inmates view movies, or on their job sites. They also meet during religious services and in the recreation yard. At Auburn, the recreation yard was huge, and inmates from all of the cellblocks went there to exercise and, more important, socialize.

There's an assortment of social activity in the Big Yard that consists of more than lifting weights and staring at the guards in the gun towers. Much information can be gained just by watching who's talking to whom. These social interactions can be defined by race, type of crime, or by mutually beneficial endeavors, such as drug dealing.

The visiting room is another place of social interaction. At Auburn during the time when Saleh was incarcerated, an inmate could receive visitors seven days a week. If a convict was jail-wise, he could have two female visitors come to the facility on the same day—one to visit him and the second, ostensibly, to visit his associate in another cellblock. Since the prison visiting room was open for six hours or more, he then had ample time to communicate directly with the other inmate on matters of importance. The system was so loose that it allowed a visitor to see more than one inmate on a single day simply by going out of the visiting room and re-registering at the facility lobby for another inmate as long as it was done before the visiting hours were over. Yousef Saleh used this method to introduce one of his visitors to Zaben. Her name was Isabel Oviedo.

It was also in Auburn prison, investigators believe, that Yousef Saleh introduced Zaben to a woman who became an important link in Zaben's outside communication system. Saleh knew that she was committed to the Palestinian movement and that she would want to meet another inmate from the West Bank. At the time, Israel and the Palestinian Authority were arguing intensely over the latter's failure to arrest suspected or known terrorists. Tensions were high.

In addition to Saleh, this woman visited one other inmate faithfully over many years, eventually becoming his appointments secretary. No one had permission to visit him unless that person first called her and scheduled a date. This inmate was domestic terrorist and Weather Underground member David Gilbert. She had visited, taken phone calls, sent money, relayed messages, and performed other services for the noted author and celebrity for almost twenty years. She has been his vital link to the outside world and the future of his movement. And by his own admission, he does have a "movement." Gilbert has not sat still while in prison these many years. He authored several books and endorsed causes. In his book *No Surrender: Writings of an Anti-Imperialist Political Prisoner*, he outlines his objective of forming an underground movement in prison, as well as offering sage advice to the new, up-and-coming domestic terrorist groups or, as Gilbert prefers to call them, the "resistance movement."[9]

Investigators found that it made sense that if Gilbert were offering advice to young radicals, there would be some who would take him up on it. They took all the visiting records of the inmates of interest, including Saleh, Zaben, Rashid, and Gilbert, and began looking for a common thread. They compared them with their phone records and financial transactions to see if there were any connections or associations with the outside world that should be of concern. What investigators found were more than fifteen men and women, mostly between the ages of twenty and twenty-eight, who were affiliated with almost two dozen politically active and sometimes subversive groups. These included the Anarchist Black Cross movement, the Animal Liberation Front (ALF), and the Earth Liberation Front (ELF). The last two have been identified by the FBI as having been involved in criminal acts of arson and violence as a means of protest. The FBI has gone as far as to say that the ALF and ELF "have emerged as a serious terrorist threat." Official estimate of the cost of the damage done by these two groups is well over $40 million.[10] Theirs was a form of domestic terrorism that was not religious or Islamic in nature. Yet considering what had happened in the past between groups of diverse ideologies, investigators were concerned that having a common perceived enemy—the U.S. government—would cause a marriage of convenience between the old and new groups. Or perhaps it would give birth to a hybrid that combined environmental issues with religious ones.

Being a published author, Gilbert attracted young, inspiring writers to come and sit at his feet, so to speak, in the prison visiting room. One of the aspirants was a college student, Dan Berger. Originally from Gainesville, Florida, where he worked on an anarchist newspaper, *ONWARD*, Berger claims to be a descendant of Jewish Holocaust survivors and is an avowed leader of the new anti-war movement.[11]

Investigators examining the records made note of the fact that Berger was in Gainesville from 2000 through 2003, the same years as Edwin Lemmons, Zaben's Hamas protégé. Preparing to write, Berger spent extensive time with Gilbert both in the visiting room and on the phone picking his brain regarding the past and the future. The result was a book that provided a glowing account of the Weather Underground in all its glory.[12]

But he did not stop there. In his other writings Berger revealed his allegiance to the radical Palestinian movement, going so far as to call the history in 1948 by which the nation of Israel was formed a "catastrophic event."[13] Berger was an advocate of the Palestine Solidarity Movement, which has been criticized by some, including Israeli intelligence, as being sympathetic to Hamas, although in its own blog the PSM has denounced violence.[14] However, some nonviolent protest movements have been known to change into aggressively violent terrorist cells. Take, for example, the members of the anti-war movement that became the Weathermen and then the Weather Underground. Could it happen again, and if so, was it necessary to monitor the members' writings and speeches to discern a shift in action? Officials overwhelmingly have said yes, even when required to walk the very thin line between civil liberties and the right to free speech on one side and legitimate security concerns on the other. The FBI was one organization that had learned firsthand the consequences of stepping over that line.[15] In addition, New York authorities were under the consent decree of the Handschu decision, which governed when and how they could investigate political or religious organizations.[16]

At least ten other individuals who had ties to radical organizations like the Anarchist Black Cross visited and communicated with David Gilbert by way of his "secretary." Often, because there were so many who wanted to visit him at the same time, she gave them alternative dates, as there are limits to the number of visitors an inmate can receive. Many of these same visitors are to this day in contact with David Gilbert and other incarcerated domestic terrorists.

In the majority of cases, visitors are a lifeline to the world for inmates, a very important and positive experience. They can help to establish and maintain family and community ties with those in prison. They also offer insight.

An inmate's visiting record can offer a unique look into his world. Some inmates receive a lot of visits at the beginning of their bids. Later on, visitations become less frequent and sometimes cease altogether. That inmate often loses hope, as he has no one waiting for him on the outside—no one to tell him what's going on back home, no one to take a message to his ex-wife or to his child. That isolation leads to the inmate becoming just another number, even to himself. Of all the privileges an inmate receives in prison, the one he fears losing the most is his visitation rights. A convict would rather be placed in a special housing unit cell for twenty-four hours a day, shipped off to Attica, lose his commissary, phones, or recreation privileges, or be fed bread and water rather than forfeit visitation rights. They are that important.

For more than twenty-five years and from all over the world, David Gilbert has received numerous visitors. He has also made a lot of phone calls. In every inmate phone booth there is a sign right above the phone in English and Spanish in big bold letters stating "All Calls Are Subject to Monitoring." Unfortunately for them, inmates don't always pay attention to the sign. And that comes back to haunt them.

This was the case with Donald "Sly" Green, an inmate in Shawangunk state prison, who was charged with directing a narcotics trafficking organization and ordering murders from his cell. He had made the mistake of making most of his deals on the prison phone. When prosecutors played the recorded phone conversations at his trial, he objected, stating, "They said 'monitor,' not 'record'!" Needless to say, his objection was overruled. The recordings were admitted as evidence, which led to his conviction for violating the Racketeering and Influence Corruption Organization (RICO) law.[17]

Gilbert has more intelligence than Sly, but he still made mistakes on the phone. There are several tape recordings of him in 2004 placing calls to Rashid Khalidi, a renowned professor of modern Arab studies at Columbia University. Immediately following the announcement of his appointment to a high academic position was an outcry of protests because of his views on the Middle East. Khalidi is an active supporter of the Palestinian cause and vocal critic of Israeli policy toward groups like Hamas.[18]

Gilbert's prison phone calls, which were recorded in the Inspector General's Office in Albany, were forwarded to investigators assigned to Operation Hades in New York City. One reason was that Gilbert was a central monitoring case, and in the normal course of department activity he was to be closely observed. Second, he had previous telephone security infractions in Attica, where a member of the prison clergy assisted him in making unmonitored calls.[19] During one of these calls to Khalidi's home, investigators heard several people using the phone to discuss the upcoming Republican National Convention in New York City and the situation developing in Iraq. Among those talking to Gilbert were two convicted domestic terrorists and several Iraqi nationals. Listening to the voices and the flow of the conversations of the parties involved, investigators came to believe that Kathy Boudin was in Khalidi's house at the time. Boudin was another member of the Weather Underground who had been convicted, along with Gilbert, for the 1981 Brinks robbery. Boudin had been released recently from Bedford Correctional Facility in Westchester County and was under strict parole supervision with restrictions on contact with convicted felons. She faced severe penalties, including immediate return to prison, if they were violated. For that reason she would not directly speak with Gilbert on the phone, but the others verbally acknowledged her presence in the house. The talk centered on tactics that should be used by the demonstrators attending the convention and protesting the war in Iraq.[20]

As the FBI and the NYPD prepared security measures for the convention, the whole nexus of these relationships between the past and the future came to the forefront. The convention was scheduled to take place at Madison Square Garden. Preparations, which included intelligence work, surveillances, and dossiers on individuals of significant interest, began long before. During these preparations, an investigator from Operation Hades spoke to Deputy Commissioner David

Cohen, Deputy Chief John Cutter, and Lt. John Bilich about another political convention fraught with subversive violence and anarchy: the Democratic National Convention in Chicago in 1968.

During the intelligence preparation for the New York convention, authorities discovered that ELF, ALF, and the Anarchist Black Cross, among others, had sent representatives to meet with the incarcerated domestic terrorists of the '60s—those who had led the violent demonstrations in Chicago. They visited not only David Gilbert but also Robert Seth Hayes and Herman Bell.[21] Some of the members of the New Age radical movement had already demonstrated a willingness to commit acts of domestic terrorism during the WTO Global Economic Conference held in Seattle in 1999 and had been observed meeting with older imprisoned radicals to discuss operational tactics. The domestic terrorists from the past were also making phone calls to the radicals of the present, discussing what to do and what not to do during the RNC convention. At one point the old-timers were overheard saying, "Learn from us."

One of the many factors that made the new radical leaders so interesting was their age. They were very young in comparison with the convicted terrorists—a generation removed. The distance they were willing to travel to visit the inmates was noteworthy. They traveled from Florida, Pennsylvania, California, Massachusetts, and Canada to several New York State prisons to visit with past members of the Weather Underground and the BLA. Intelligence folders were created on each one of the visitors as well as the organizations they represented. This information was then used by NYPD and the FBI during the convention to disrupt demonstrations planned by the groups. During the protests, undercover officers approached these individuals in the crowd, called them by name, and asked where the meetings to plan the demonstrations were being held. This completely surprised the young radicals. They had survived on anonymity, wearing masks or bandanas to hide their identities when demonstrations turned violent, as they did in Seattle. The authorities' tactic caused them to abandon previously planned vandalism for fear their identities were already known.

This intelligence developed by members of Operation Hades is credited with having prevented numerous violent acts during the convention, although in 2005 the existence of the intelligence folders was a part of a federal lawsuit brought against the NYPD by the ACLU and lawyers for the protesters, charging a violation of the Handschu Decision.[22] The lawsuit is ongoing.

Regardless, in trying to unravel the web of relationships between the past, present, and future terrorists, Operation Hades found that the process of radicalization is cyclical. The past influences the present and most likely the future. This is particularly true in the prison environment where individuals like Yousef Saleh and Abdel Zaben were able to interact frequently with incarcerated domestic terrorists from the 1960s and their new disciples—the radicals of the twenty-first century.

CHAPTER 7

Operation Hades

The year 1999 was a benchmark in gauging the threat of radical Islam to the United States. It was sandwiched between two years with major terrorist incidents: 1998, with the al Qaeda bombings of two U.S. embassies in Africa and 2000, when al Qaeda bombed the USS *Cole* in Yemen. It ended with the arrest of Ahmed Ressam, an al Qaeda operative plotting to blow up Los Angeles International Airport on New Year's Eve. Those 365 days contained several key indicators of foreign involvement in prison radicalization.

In the aftermath of the September 11 attacks, President George W. Bush and Congress established a commission to study the events leading up to them. The goal of the commission was to detail what mistakes had been made and what actions would be necessary to prevent future attacks. The commission's final report was published July 22, 2004. It contained several significant comments regarding 1999, including the observation that Ressam's "millennium plotting in Canada in 1999 may have been part of Bin Laden's first serious attempt to implement a terrorist strike in the U.S."[1] It then went on to say that "we detailed various missed opportunities" to thwart the 9/11 attacks.[2] It outlined the reasons for those missed opportunities, basically that information was not shared, analysis was not pooled, and effective operations were not launched. Committee members went on record saying, "Often the handoffs of information were lost across the divide separating . . . agencies of the government."[3] They also cited a significant yet little known report regarding terrorist recruitment efforts:

"A clandestine source said in 1998 that a Bin Ladin cell in New York was recruiting Muslim-American youth for attacks."[4]

Two other incidents occurred in 1999 that, although not specifically mentioned in the *9/11 Commission Report*, were also examples of opportunities missed by the intelligence and law enforcement communities. The first occurred in February when both the FBI and the NYDOCS Inspector General's Office received information specifically detailing recruitment efforts within prison.

Confidential sources named in an FBI Automated Case Support report authored by an agent assigned to the JTTF told investigators about individuals associated with the plot to destroy New York City landmarks and their association with a Saudi-Arabian inmate in a maximum-security prison in New York.[5] The case was dubbed Terror Stop.[6] The report went on to mention that the inmate, along with several members of a domestic terrorist organization already serving time in the same facility for the Brinks robbery, had formed an alliance. One of the confidential sources said that this alliance had a singular goal. It "was tasked with training incarcerated members to work with Middle Eastern Muslims to perform acts of Jihad."[7]

The source also informed authorities of the name the group had chosen for itself—the Talem Circle. This name had been used before in the prison Muslim community to define the select group of individuals who were responsible for the security and intelligence operations of the mosque. Additional information from one of the sources in the report also revealed a plot to kill a New York civil service employee and a Muslim clergyman. At the time the FBI was told of the threat against the imam, he was working in a maximum-security prison north of New York City.

Neither the FBI nor the Inspector General's Office actively pursued the information received. It was simply filed away in the ACS report. The investigator from NYDOCS never informed the inspector general of the allegations. The cleric, a government employee, was a Pakistani national and Sunni Muslim who had been hired by Warith Deen Umar in 1992. According to one inmate source, he was not fully supportive of the radical Islamic recruitment efforts and therefore had been targeted for removal. He was never notified of the threat on his life.[8] However, in March 2003 the imam again became a subject of interest to investigators because of his travels to Pakistan and a possible association with Jamaat al Dawa, an Islamic terrorist group associated with al Qaeda in Kashmir.

Three years after 9/11, this ACS report again surfaced. Members of Operation Hades asked the NYDOCS investigator about the information in the report. His initial response was to deny ever receiving the information. Later, when confronted with the documentation from the ACS file, he amended his story and stated that he did indeed receive the information and had conducted his own investigation without notifying his supervisor. However, upon request, he was not able to produce the case folder detailing the results of his research.

Even if he had attempted to look into the allegations as he claimed he had, this particular investigator lacked the resources and the expertise to investigate issues of international terrorism. His main function in the Inspector General's Office at that time was to supervise internal investigations of prison guards who had used excessive force on inmates—not at all connected to gathering intelligence information on international terrorism.

There was another occurrence of overlooked information approximately five months later in July 1999 when a detective in the Yonkers Police Department received information from a confidential informant regarding terrorist recruitment efforts in prison. The informant had an interesting pedigree. He was a convicted sex offender recently released from prison and at various times an outlaw biker, a Native American shaman, and a Buddhist monk. He was most recently a convert to Islam who claimed sheikh status in the Muslim community in New York City. Despite the checkered past of this particular source, his information was still considered significant enough to be put into the report:

> Abdel Nasser Zaben, Jordanian-born inmate, who had identified himself as a follower of Osama Bin Laden, spoke of Jihad and dying for the cause of Islam. Abdel said his group was interested in recruiting inmates in United States Prisons that were disgruntled with America and soon to be released. His group would have them trained in the Middle East and return to the United States to participate in a Jihad.[9]

During their time at Fishkill, Zaben had told the informant about several former inmates who were already participating in the training that he had helped facilitate overseas in madrassas and various camps. The source also spoke knowingly of the Muslim community in the prison, as he had regularly attended Jummah services in the prison mosque and taken part in other activities with Muslim inmates. He then spoke about the community, about who was really in charge of it, and about the relationship between Zaben and the civilian imam, Salahuddin Muhammad.

As the informant's release date from prison approached, he was preparing to re-enter society by trying to find gainful employment and a place to live. During that time, Zaben came to his cell privately and gave him specific instructions to follow when he was released. He was directed to go to the Al Taqwa mosque on Bedford Avenue in Brooklyn, where he would make contact with other former inmates who were members of that congregation.

After his release in August 1999, the source received letters from Zaben directing him to go hear Sheikh Muhammad Hassan speak at Madison Square Garden. The sheikh, also known as Mohammed Mohammed Hassan El Shariff, was a noted Egyptian cleric who had arrived in the United States in 1995 to take over the Abu Bakr mosque in New York after the indictment and arrested of the Blind Sheikh Abdel Rahman. The informant was further instructed by Zaben to arrive early and that someone would meet him and take him to be introduced to the sheikh. Authorities believed that event to have been the Islamic Holy Life rally held on August 14, 1999, featuring such other speakers as Wagdy Ghazawie, Hamza Youssef, and Zaid Shaakr, and sponsored by Sirhaj Wahhaj, the imam from the Al Taqwa mosque.

The significance of these specific instructions from Zaben should not be overlooked. At that time, it was almost unfathomable that an inmate in prison would have the prestige to arrange a personal meeting with Hassan. It perfectly demonstrated the prison subculture's network system (at the time, run by Zaben) and its influence on events outside the prison walls. It also would become the benchmark for gauging the relationship between radical Islamic fundamentalists and the prison subculture.

The detective from the Yonkers Police Department who received this information did the right thing by reporting it to the JTTF office in New York City. The FBI reacted in two ways: it directed the informant not to attend the meeting with Hassan, and it sent two agents from the JTTF to Fishkill to speak with Zaben. During this visit, one of the agents asked Zaben, "Are you a terrorist?" He answered, "No." Report filed. Case closed.

No vetting was done on Abdel Nasser Zaben. There was no analysis of the information available from NYDOC's records. Data that was readily available and that would have provided insight into Zaben's relationships with the clergy, visitors, and former inmates, along with his financial transaction history, was never requested by JTTF agents. Three years later, one of the investigators who conducted that interview with Zaben in Fishkill was asked by members of Operation Hades to produce a copy of his report. He said he couldn't find it but believed it was somewhere in a warehouse in Washington, D.C., along with other JTTF records.

Immediately following 9/11, the NYPD, to its credit, revisited a number of old leads regarding terrorism and terrorist contacts. This particular lead came to the surface. However, the NYPD at that time did not have the expertise or logistical support necessary to probe the criminal subculture in prisons outside the New York City area, and the network of information sharing between various investigative agencies was informal and fragile at best. There were turf wars, diametrically opposed interests, and outright refusals by the FBI, CIA, NYPD, New York State Police, and NYDOCS to grant access to information. The informal relationships that existed were only built on old-school camaraderie and handshakes, often at an after-hours watering hole for those "on the job."

Enter Chauncey Parker. Appointed director of the New York State Division of Criminal Justice Services in 2002 by Governor George Pataki, he had the authority to make both the state and city criminal justice agencies work together in a way that hadn't happened previously. In addition to being "criminal justice czar," Parker was appointed by the White House Office of Drug Policy as the director of the New York and New Jersey High-Intensity Drug Trafficking Area (HIDTA) office. HIDTA was originally set up as an intelligence-sharing organization consisting of federal, state, and local agencies in an effort to make an impact on the war on drugs. With these dual roles, Parker had the backing of both the president of the United States and the governor of New York.

Parker searched for innovative ways to reduce crime and its effects and was a motivating visionary when it came to bringing people and agencies together for a common goal, which was often a logistical nightmare. Agency heads or their subordinates argued over where to meet or work, as well as over silly issues like who sat where, which could torpedo an honorable initiative. One of his solutions was to create the Regional Intelligence Center. In the initial stages, it was simply home to HIDTA and the NYPD Intelligence Division but eventually became much more. It was the first of its kind in the United States.

The first issue was where to put the center's offices. As a result of 9/11, several key government agency offices in Lower Manhattan, many of which were located at 26 Federal Plaza, had been destroyed. Because office space in New York City was not easily obtainable, the Intelligence Division of the New York City Police Department had a big problem. Their solution? Chelsea Market.

Built on the site of the old National Biscuit Building, a New York City landmark purchased in the 1990s by investor Irwin P. Cohen, Chelsea Market is located between Ninth and Tenth Avenues and Fifteenth and Sixteenth Streets in Manhattan. Rich in history and art, it comprises food courts, shops, studios, and offices. In the spirit of cooperation between government and the private sector after 9/11, Cohen wanted to help with the relocation process as soon as possible, so he offered vacant office space there to the government agencies.

Parker and John Cutter, deputy chief of NYPD's Intelligence Division under Chief Michael Tiffany, planned the design of the future headquarters of the Regional Intelligence Center. Parker's role was to bring agencies and the allocated manpower together. Cutter took on the logistical role, seeing to the physical plant, which was simply empty space, without furniture or office equipment. But it had promise. He and Parker discussed the layout of the new location down to the smallest details, like the placement and the size of the cubicle dividers. Cutter wanted the dividers smaller than what were previously used at Federal Plaza so that every detective, investigator, analyst, and agent could see and hear each other as they worked. He was definitely not an interior decorator, but he had a philosophy and theory at work in his imagination. He believed that a simple change like this would foster better communication and cooperation in Intelligence. People would share information. There would be no turf wars. And it worked.

Parker and Cutter's vision for interagency cooperation led to other agencies assigning personnel to the Regional Intelligence Center. These included the State Department, the Treasury Department, the U.S. Marshals Service, INS, the New York State Police, NYDOCS, New York State Division of Parole, Customs, and other lesser known agencies, such as the Financial Crimes Enforcement Network (FINCEN), are housed. It was a regular alphabet soup. In the buildings adjacent to Chelsea Market were the DEA's New York headquarters, with its newly formed Organized Crime Drug Enforcement Task Force (OCDETF), which began to focus on narco-terrorism finances.

Within the NYPD Intelligence Division was a group called the Field Intelligence Investigative Services (FIIS). This unit's members consisted of Lt. John Bilich, Sgt. James Murphy, and Detectives Dave Miller, Dan Coates, Ira Greenberg, Milton Lopez, James Maxson, Bill Blanderman, and Matt Rosenthal. From the NYDOCS's Office of the Inspector General came Ken Torreggiani, a specialist in the cultivation and control of human assets in the Prison Subculture Network (PSN). Cutter gave this group the task of revisiting the 1999 lead from Yonkers, under the direction of David Cohen. John Cutter was a top cop with a unique awareness and approach to combating terrorism. As he said on National Public Radio, "Look, I know we're the Police Department and we deal with crime, but terrorism is just a higher level of crime, and we have to know about it. If it's in our midst, I need somebody to investigate it."[10] He was a man ahead of his time who knew what he was talking about when it came to fighting terrorist threats in a major metropolitan area. Backing up his opinions, the RAND Corporation released a report of findings in 2008 after studying over six hundred terrorist organizations that had operated within a span of almost forty years. The study made a bold statement that "all terrorist groups eventually end," which was then followed by the question, "But how do they end?"[11] The researchers concluded that police investigative work was the most successful method in accomplishing the goal of eradicating terrorist groups:

> Against terrorist groups . . . policing is likely to be the most effective strategy. Police and Intelligence Services have better training and information to penetrate and disrupt terrorist organizations than do such institutions as the military. . . . Local police . . . usually have a permanent presence in cities, towns, and villages; a better understanding of the threat environment in these areas; and better human intelligence.[12]

Cutter was an integral part of the Intelligence Division but not the head of it. At the time, David Cohen was the deputy commissioner of intelligence for the NYPD. He was appointed to that position in 2002 by

Mayor Michael Bloomberg after being chosen by NYPD commissioner Ray Kelly. Prior to that, Cohen worked for the CIA for over thirty-five years, advancing from the rank of analyst to deputy director of operations. The 9/11 Commission lauded him as the man who had the foresight to start a unit whose sole responsibility was the investigation of one individual, Osama bin Laden.[13] That was five years prior to 9/11.

Like anyone in public office, Cohen also had critics. Some thought he was unwilling to share control and would bend investigative intelligence reports to fit the political desires of his superiors. Two specific criticisms of Cohen's analytical track record were expounded on by former CIA agent Ralph McGehee. He believed that during the Vietnam Conflict, CIA analysts such as Cohen had manipulated the casualty figures to show that America was winning. During the 1980s, Cohen oversaw the agency's analysis of Eastern Bloc influence. McGehee believed that following Mehmet Ali Agca's attempted assignation of Pope John Paul II in 1981, the agency was longing for a connection with the Soviets. McGehee and others, citing the report of the "Cowey Panel," which was commissioned by CIA director Robert Gates to look into the initial intelligence report on the assassination, have claimed that certain CIA analysts, Cohen one of them, deliberately slanted their analysis in an attempt to support a theory that the Soviet KGB was involved. He did this, according to McGehee, because that was the prevailing wind in the political hierarchy of the agency at the time.[14] According to one reporter's exposé, "CIA analysts found themselves under severe pressure to conform to the administration's political desires, especially hyping the Soviet strategic threat and blaming virtually all acts of terrorism on Moscow."[15] Other critics claimed Cohen had no operational experience, that he was an analyst who only through his political savvy made it to the top of the Operations Directorate.[16] In the shadowy world of intelligence, you often make more enemies than friends.

Regardless, David Cohen brought an entirely different approach to the melding of police work and intelligence in the war on terrorism. Shortly after his appointment the NYPD sought the assistance of the Inspector General's Office in identifying the inmates involved in the alleged radical Islamic recruitment effort. At that point, all the NYPD had to go on was the name of a single inmate, Abdel Nasser Zaben. No other associates or recruits had been identified. By this time, Zaben had been in prison for more than nine years, and the number of individuals he had contact with—including inmates, clergy, and others—was enormous and continuing to grow.

The volume of data on Zaben was tremendous and would take a Herculean effort to collect, analyze, and disseminate. It would also require assistance from international agencies because of Zaben's contacts outside the United States. This gave birth to the multifaceted investigative group of agents and analysts that was Operation Hades. That name was chosen by the NYPD Intelligence Unit for a couple of reasons. The first was the necessity to give every investigation a catchy name. Old habits die hard. The second was that they thought prison was a version of Hell and that Operation Hades sounded much better than "Operation Hell." I doubt any considered at the time the writings of the fourteenth-century Italian author Dante Alighieri and his nine circles of Hell outlined in *The Inferno*.

As with all complex endeavors, great minds are needed. Unfortunately, great minds often come with big egos that can shipwreck any journey. And so it was when intelligence officials sought to put in place a mechanism that could identify possible terrorist recruitment efforts and gauge the level of radical Islam in prison. That operation was almost ended before it even began because of the egos.

Chauncey Parker had scheduled a meeting among the various government agencies to determine what sources of information were available to all the agencies involved and to set up a formal protocol for cooperation. In dealing with multiple agencies, it is necessary to understand that each one is different from the others in operational procedures and, more important, in operational philosophy. If anything was learned from the *9/11 Commission Report*, it was that the failure to identify sources of information was an issue and, even greater, that the sharing of the information between the concerned agencies was vital.

The meeting did not begin well. I remember hearing, "This is bullshit! We're out of here! Who do they [NYPD] think they are? The colonel from the state police is here and he's getting stood up because Cohen and Cutter are busy!" And with that statement, the group that I had walked into the Regional Intelligence Center with—Inspector Bart Johnson, Col. Pedro Perez from the New York State Police, and Inspector General Richard Roy from NYDOCS—stormed out.

I was left standing alone in the room with John Bilich, the commanding lieutenant of the NYPD Field Intelligence Investigative Services, a branch within the Intelligence Division. For a moment, we tried to figure out what had gone wrong and how to fix it. I told him we would be across the street getting something to eat, and he said he would find Cutter in the meantime. Two hours later, Lieutenant Bilich brought Chief Cutter into a Dominican restaurant on Ninth Avenue where we were finishing lunch. For the next hour, he apologized, humored us, and soothed the bruised egos. Then he picked up the check. We were back on track.

A memorandum of understanding was drafted that identified what seemed to some a most unlikely source of information in the war on terrorism, the New York State prison system. Prison has been called a lot of things—penitentiary, correctional facility, slammer, farm, belly of the beast, stir—just to name a few. It is probably closer in analogy to Hell for several reasons. It is indeed a place where hope is abandoned, and as Dante described, there are different levels depending on an individual's sins/crimes. For example, doing time in Attica was vastly different from working the horse farm in Wallkill Correctional Facility. Inmates try to work their way up to another level out of the abyss, passing each other as they pay for their crimes. It is also a place, like Dante's allegory, where the residents interact with each other in different ways and for different purposes. The official goal is confinement or removal from society. The desired goal is rehabilitation. The reality is neither.

Prison can also be a wealth of knowledge and enlightenment. Where else can a two-bit burglar learn to become an international jewel thief, or a purse-snatcher evolve into a weapons procurement financier? But it's a two-way street, and cops can learn, too, if they know where and how to look.

This very notion was the key to the confidential intelligence investigation. The members of Operation Hades journeyed into the multilayered realm of darkness where the imprisoned dwelled. And like Dante, the investigators sometimes encountered individuals who were beyond logic and belief.

The goal of the operation was to determine the level, if any, of radical Islamic recruitment in the prison culture and beyond. Why beyond? Simply put, inmates do not live in a vacuum. Gone are the days when they were locked up and the key was thrown away. Convicts today are not isolated from society. They have significant influence and contact with the outside world and the outside world with them. The walls of the modern-day prison are porous.

It has been said by noted counterterrorism expert Marc Sageman that the majority of the young up-and-coming jihadists lack leadership and structure.[17] This is not the case in the prison subculture. It has its own leadership network, both within and outside the walls, and is well structured. Part of its structure is a communication system that allows its members to give direction, issue orders, and obtain and allocate financial resources among prisons, cities, and—in the case of Zaben—countries.

Two prime examples of the intricacies and abilities of the Prison Subculture Network (PSN) to reach beyond the prison walls are the cases of the aforementioned Donald "Sly" Green and Luis Felipe, also known as King Blood. Green was the head of the LA Boys, a Buffalo street gang. While beginning to serve his sentence of twenty-five years to life in 1989 for second-degree murder, he met Carlos Herrera, a Colombian drug lord. Herrera was also serving a sentence of twenty-five to life but for sale of a controlled substance. A marriage of convenience then took place, as Sly had the street network contacts and Carlos had the international connections for drugs.

Together, with the help of other inmates and visitors, they orchestrated narcotics trafficking and money laundering, and ordered murders from their cells in Shawangunk Correctional Facility. Green used prison phones, visitors, mail, and the inmate commissary and accounting system to run a continuing criminal enterprise. Lt. Ed Tasker of NYDOCS gave the FBI more than a thousand recordings of conversations that helped in the indictment and conviction of twenty-six defendants.[18]

Details of the second case demonstrating the effectiveness of the PSN revealed how the Almighty Latin Kings Nation, a street gang originating in a Chicago jail, had developed and grown as a continuing criminal enterprise in the New York State prison system. In 1986, Luis Felipe was a twenty-one-year-old from the Bronx serving a sentence at Collins Correctional Facility, just outside Buffalo, of three to nine years for manslaughter. He was transferred later on to Attica state prison. While incarcerated, he and others conspired to commit armed robbery, narcotics trafficking, and murder.

His preferred method of communication with the members of his organization was the PSN's underground mail system, which helped inmates smuggle secret communiqués to members who were in other prisons or on the street. Visitors often acted as couriers and in some extreme cases so did NYDOCS employees and volunteers.

Felipe used this system to order the murder of rivals and insubordinate members of the Latin Kings. His edicts reached through prison walls and across state lines. The FBI and the NYPD's Major Case Squad were given the bulk of the credit for dismantling this criminal enterprise and solving the numerous associated homicide cases. The truth was, however, that an individual named Richard Roy—then the NYDOCS director of crisis intervention—had come forth to NYPD with recovered letters from Felipe outlining the murders. At the time, Roy was gathering intelligence on prison gangs and had ordered that a mail watch be placed on King Blood. Looking strictly from a prison management perspective, prison officials were attempting to prohibit unauthorized groups (such as the Latin Kings) from disrupting the good running order of the prison. The feds and the cops were looking solely at the streets. No one was seeing the big picture.

After Felipe's conviction on RICO charges in U.S. District Court, the sentencing judge, realizing the power and magnitude of the PSN, placed strict controls on his contacts after he was transferred to the custody of the Federal Bureau of Prisons. In essence, this prohibited him from visitors, phone calls, or written communication without the prior knowledge and approval of the court.

Although admirable, this method, known as Special Administrative Measures (SAMs) is not foolproof. Consider the case of Abdel Rahman, the Blind Sheikh. He had been convicted for the first attack on the World Trade Center, as well as for conspiring to destroy several landmarks in the New York City area. At his sentencing, the judge placed SAMs on his communications with the outside world. Unfortunately, that didn't work. In 2002, his attorney, Lynne Stewart, and two others were arrested and charged with smuggling coded messages out of the prison from Rahman to other members of his organization elsewhere.[19] Stewart and her codefendants, Mohamed Yousry and Ahmed Sattar, were found guilty of conspiracy, providing material support to a terrorist, and defrauding the government. She received a sentence of twenty-eight months and, after exhausting her appeals, was taken into custody of the Federal Bureau of Prisons. Stewart became just another inmate with a number and is currently serving her time at the Metropolitan Correctional Center in Lower Manhattan, not far from the site of the World Trade Center. Once again, terrorists and inmates had demonstrated their adaptability to their environment. In the words of the oft-repeated proverb, "Where there is a will, there is a way."

The intricacy and importance of the inmate communication structure has been best described by those with experience in this arena. Richard B. Zabel, a former head of the narcotics unit in the U.S. Attorney's Office, said that inmates in New York had developed highly effective communication systems, often leveraging the various religious opportunities within prison. In the past, he said, members of the Latin Kings, for example, met in the prison chapel and transmitted messages—both inside and outside the prison—using Bibles.[20]

All of these cases come to an interesting point of connection, as Abdel Nasser Zaben was an inmate in the prison system when most of these things were going on. Because no one lives in a vacuum, to be successful a new convict must observe those around him and learn how to do time. A jihadist born in a foreign country can be put in a prison system in the United States. At first, he doesn't know how to tie his shoes without bending down and exposing his ass. But as he listens, he learns, and as he meets others, he is shown how the PSN operates, complete with codes, kited letters, visitors, three-way phone calls, disbursements, sympathetic employees, and volunteers.

The jihadist does not have to build his own network from the ground up. He simply needs to adapt the existing system to his cause. This was exactly what Zaben did during the years he was incarcerated in New York State. Only a prison specialist could explain it to the outside law enforcement and intelligence community.

I had been assigned to the Regional Intelligence Center in New York by NYDOCS commissioner Glenn Goord prior to Operation Hades and had spent time talking to the members of FIIS about the environment of prison and its subculture. Wanting to learn, they were like sponges soaking up as much as they could about the PSN and its influence. A few weeks after our initial briefings, I walked into an office in Chelsea Market where Chief Cutter and Commanding Lieutenant Bilich were speaking with a gentleman in civilian clothes. They were explaining to him the details they were learning about Zaben and about an inmate's ability to not only survive but thrive in the prison subculture. After the briefing the somewhat unassuming, scholarly-looking person said, "What we need to do is hire a consultant who will be able to speak about this prison phenomenon in depth." Hearing this, I remarked, "Hey, what am I, chopped liver? Why do you think I was sent here?"

As I stormed out of the room, I turned to Bilich and said, "Who does that guy think he is?" He replied, "Pat, I'd like you to meet Deputy

Commissioner David Cohen." And that rough introduction was the beginning of the melding of corrections, police, and intelligence personnel.

Accomplishing the mission of Operation Hades required a multifaceted approach from federal, state, and city resources, all thinking outside of the "cell," so to speak. The operation drew on international resources as well, with assistance provided from such members of the worldwide community as Scotland Yard, the Canadian intelligence services, and the Toronto Police Department.

The men and women who worked on this intelligence operation were uniquely talented individuals with a sense of humor and the intuition necessary to work on this type of investigation. It was a diverse consortium. Streetwise detectives were paired with cultural analysts, prison specialists with CIA field operatives, and parole officers with Arabic translators.

At the onset, two key questions arose: who were the inmates sent outside the United States, and who was Abdel Nasser Zaben? In order to answer the second question, experts knew they would need to sift through every piece of datum about him, including his INS folder and his prison records. The NYDOCS has a state-of-the-art information management system. It was one of the first in the nation to keep automated records on every prison where an inmate was ever incarcerated, who were his cell mates, what were his programs, who visited him, and what his telephone records revealed. In addition, officials researched his correspondence, financial transactions, job assignments, enemies, unusual incidents, medical records, IQ test results, religious affiliation, program assignments, and much more. The Inspector General's Office provided this data to all the member agencies working in Operation Hades. Besides being responsible for investigating crimes committed within the prison system, the office oversees intelligence collection, analysis, and dissemination within the prison system and had in fact developed many of the data collection systems tools in the Operation Hades investigative process. These tools were used to interdict narcotics, prevent escapes, and root out corruption. In addition, the Inspector General's Office was a key contributor to the U.S. attorney's successful prosecution of the persons responsible for the first World Trade Center attack. Brian F. Malone, inspector general from 1978 to 2001, was instrumental as well in the FBI's case against Edmund Wilson, the rogue CIA agent convicted of selling plastic explosives to the Libyans. Given its history, the office was and continues to be a fully competent player in the intelligence arena.

It's difficult to describe the enormous volume of data records that had to be reviewed and analyzed by members of Operation Hades. As mentioned earlier, more than 110,000 inmates annually pass through Rikers Island alone, the main feeder for the New York State prison system—not to mention that the facility has about 30,000 visitors and 250,000 telephone calls and financial transactions totaling in excess of $25 million that are made there each year. To make matters even more complicated, Zaben had been in prison for nine years.

Every name, phone number, address, or organization ever connected to Zaben in any way over that period was combed through, sifted, strained, and regurgitated five times over. Link charts and matrix diagrams were constructed in an attempt to explain the intricate relationships of convicts, visitors, clergy, volunteers, and members of suspected organizations. Investigators and Arabic translators listened to hours upon hours of recorded phone conversations. As they navigated through that sea of minutiae, investigators learned that in addition to inmate Edwin Lorenzo Lemmons, others had become disciples and sent out on missions. Some were picked up in far-off places such as North Africa. Others never made it out of the Bronx.

At the beginning of Operation Hades, only a handful of individuals believed it had value. Some agencies thought it was an exercise in futility. However, as soon as the results of the operation started to come to fruition, and the impact that the information being collected, analyzed, and evaluated could have in the war on radical Islam was realized, everybody wanted in. Requests came not only from the United States but around the world for a look at how the system worked. Scotland Yard extolled its virtues and eventually copied it. Brian Jenkins, a counterterrorism expert from the prestigious RAND Corporation, had high praise for its ability to uncover a radical Islamic recruitment effort. The CIA wanted to use the information for cultivating potential human assets to send overseas to such places as Afghanistan, Iran, Iraq, and Somalia. They were, in essence, competing for the same young, impressionable, malleable recruits that the terrorist recruiters seek."[21]

Then the fights and the hostile takeover attempts came. The Justice Department wanted overall access to the information systems, not a partnership. The NYDOCS did not want to give carte blanche access, fearing that if another agency, like the FBI, uncovered corruption or crime in a prison, they would not notify NYDOCS so it could be dealt with through normal procedures without embarrassing the governor's office. The NYPD had an ongoing feud with the Feds since the first World Trade Center bombing in 1993 and did not want to concede authority for intelligence that might affect New York City. Even Deputy Commissioner Cohen himself had a long history of disdain for the FBI when it came to intelligence operations.[22]

Eventually Chauncey Parker, Police Commissioner Ray Kelly, and Corrections Commissioner Glenn Goord became instrumental in resolving the issues, and all agencies were brought in under the umbrella of the JTTF's Correctional Intelligence Initiative program. In 2006 investigators from the Inspector General's Office and NYPD detectives were given permanent seats on the panel that oversaw the collection, analysis, and dissemination of intelligence gathered from the prison system. Security clearances were granted to investigators working Operation Hades and confidentiality agreements were signed.

The goal of this new program was that, working together proactively, federal, state, and city investigators would continue to monitor radical Islamic recruitment efforts. When threats were found, they would have the ability and authority to close down the cell.

CHAPTER 8

Closing the Cell Door

"When you walk down the gallery, grab each cell by the bars, and rattle it twice to make sure it's locked." With these words a seasoned veteran corrections officer instructs a rookie on how to do his count during lock-in. He finishes the lesson with these sage words: "If they ain't locked, they ain't in." In all of prison, there is no sound more ominous to a convict's ear than the sound of a cell door slamming shut.

Operation Hades began the process of closing down the recruitment cells with the exposure of Abdel Zaben's network. As the new national cooperation program began to take over, the effectiveness was seen almost immediately.

In the spring of 2004, inmate JMC (full name redacted), also known as Hakeem Mujaheed, was picked up by U.S. agents in northeastern Africa while attempting to join an Islamic terrorist group.[1] As he was debriefed by intelligence officers, his story gave an inside view of the full process of radicalization starting within the prison walls, moving to U.S. cities and then abroad.

JMC was born in New York City in 1972. His father was a New York City police officer. He grew up in an abusive home until the rage inside of him burst forth and he shot and killed his father with his own police-issued gun in June 1992. Because of the extenuating circumstances and a sympathetic judge, the charges were reduced from murder to manslaughter and he received a sentence of three to nine years in prison. Like so many, he converted to Islam while in a New York State prison, attended the prison mosque, and got to know several chaplains, including Zakee Abdul Hameed, who had been hired in 1990 by Warith Deen Umar. Hameed had worked in several state prisons in upstate New York and had access to and influence over various inmates.

In January 1998, JMC was paroled from Queensboro Correctional Facility. He completed his parole supervision in December 2001, three months after 9/11. Prior to his release, he had been encouraged by prison chaplains to attend Jummah services with Umar and Hameed at selected mosques in New York City, including Taha on Nassau Road in Roosevelt, New York, a hamlet on Long Island. He was also directed to Al Taqwa on Bedford Avenue in Brooklyn. After completing his training there, JMC, now using his Islamic name, Hakeem Mujaheed, went to Norfolk, Virginia, and attended the mosque on Granby Street.

In an arranged meeting that took place at this same mosque, Hakeem was introduced to another former New York inmate, James Lewis. Lewis had a history of violence and involvement with weapons and had been in and out of the prison system for twenty years. During his third period of incarceration, he converted to Islam and became a fervent Salafist, taking the name of Zaiky Abdul-Malik. Agents from the Joint Terrorist Task Force observed Lewis entering and leaving at least five different mosques known to have ties to such radical Islamic teachers as Anwar Al-Awlaki.

Both Hakeem and Lewis were reported to be attending the various mosques in the greater Hampton Roads area, as well as studying at an Islamic center farther north in Falls Church, Virginia. While in Falls Church, Hakeem was provided with contacts and locations abroad where he could continue his Islamic studies and training to become fully committed to the jihad. Had he not been intercepted by U.S. agents, he probably would have become another martyr in the cause of Allah. In this case, the cooperation between the CIA, JTTF, and the NYPD Intelligence Division was able to close the door on this recruit before he could do damage.[2]

In light of the specifics of the cases of Hakeem Mujaheed, the Lackawanna Six, José Padilla (the "Dirty Bomber"), and other would-be homegrown terrorists, U.S. counterterrorism officials were then and still are now on the lookout for disenfranchised young American males traveling abroad to countries of interest or "hot spots" where radical Islamic groups are known to be active in recruitment and training for acts of jihad.

The majority of these countries are in the Middle East and North Africa: Afghanistan, Pakistan, Egypt, Yemen, Somalia, and Morocco. Intelligence agencies that had cooperation agreements with foreign intelligence services were often tipped off when an American meeting the established profiles suddenly showed up in their country. Surveillance is set up on them to determine who they are attempting to contact and whether they have deviated from their stated purpose for visiting the country. Requests are sent back to the agencies in the United States that might have specific information regarding the individuals' backgrounds, information that includes their criminal history, and any prison intelligence on them.

In prison, making sure a gate or cell is locked is paramount to good security. In counterterrorism, the same principle can be applied. But closing the cell is one thing; keeping it closed is another.

In 2005, while Abdel Zaben was waiting to be released from Shawangunk and returned to Ramallah, he spoke with a confidential source. He told him that for the last six months he had been taking business classes and learning all about computers. When the source asked him why, he laughed and said, "You think I want to be a simple clerk?"[3]

He then went on to detail his plans for the future. Zaben was very familiar with deportation proceedings and knew that Immigration and Customs Enforcement and the State Department would impede his reentry into the United States. He had been down this route before in 1990, the first time he was deported. Then it only took him six months to get back into America. With this deportation, he knew it would be a more difficult but not impossible. His scheduled date for release from prison was January 25, 2005. In normal circumstances, if he were paroled to New York or to another state, he would be required to fulfill six years of supervised release or parole supervision. Supervised release to a foreign country can be a little dicey. If the country is an ally or has a cooperative criminal justice agreement with the United States, the transfer of the supervision guidelines can still be accomplished. But prison release to a country with no agreement is a joke. No requirements are placed on the ex-con. At the time of his arrest, the West Bank was under the control of the Israeli government, an ally with whom the United States has a long history of criminal justice cooperation. In 2005 when he was to be released, that same area was under the control of the Palestinian Authority, and the different factions within it, such as Al-Fatah, were fighting with Hamas for ultimate authority and control. There was no agreement for supervision of ex-convicts returned from the United States.

Zaben knew he would first be flown to Jordan, then be escorted by Jordanian security personnel across the King Hussein Bridge to the West Bank. Once across the bridge, Zaben also knew there would be no controlling authority monitoring his whereabouts and checking whether he was gainfully employed, keeping curfew, attending anger regression classes or avoiding contact with known criminals or terrorists. There would be no parole officer to whom he would be expected to account for his every movement and his acquaintances. However, for him to move outside that area to a country like Canada or a European country, he would need some bona fides for travel. To accomplish that, he planned to use his prison vocational experience to assist him. He told the confidential source that with his computer experience, he would try to gain employment with an Arabic news service. He said he needed to obtain media credentials so that he could travel freely. To him, having the credentials was like having an imam's clerk pass in prison. Both gave him greater access and ability. His goal was to return to the United States in spite of any entrance restriction. His adaptability, ingenuity, and commitment to the cause were clearly demonstrated to the source when he said, "*Enshallah*, I will return here."[4] And without vigilance and fortitude by the agencies that inherited the work of Operation Hades, it may have happened.

Operation Hades developed a system to gauge the level of radicalization of a terrorist recruitment cell, as well as the ability to identify, monitor, and neutralize it. It accomplished its goal and more. Of course, it did not entirely eradicate the problem of prison radicalization. That was not the goal of the project. I have learned over my years working in the criminal justice system that no person or project completely eradicates anything in prison. Whether it is drug use and trafficking, rape, assault, corruption, or, in this case, terrorism, these are realities of prison behavior that will continue.

For instance, take a simple task like banning cigarette smoking. Attempts to do that in prison have been met with the ingenuity of the con. In one correctional system that prohibited tobacco products in the commissary and deemed tobacco as contraband, inmates were paying employees as much as one hundred dollars a pack to smuggle them in. Administrators may seek to change prisoner behavior, but if anyone thinks complete prevention will happen in prison, he is destined for disappointment. The same goes for terrorism recruitment. If anything, Operation Hades generated a healthy discussion among law enforcement and counterterrorism experts as to the reality of the phenomenon and the level of threat that it poses.

Those two issues—the existence and the level of threat—have been debated by decent and honorable professionals in the field. There are those who say that there is no such thing as Islamic radicalization in prison. They believe that the issue has been exaggerated and that it poses no threat to the United States or the world at large. That group includes some correctional administrators and sociologists. Their position is based on discussions with prison officials and inmates around the country. They even go so far as to disconnect the released prisoners' actions from the influence of the environment from whence they came, stating, "If prisons are incubators for radicalization, you think we would have seen it by now."[5]

Other schools of thought say that the threat of Islamic radicalization in prison "is of low importance" or "a minor factor" and "relatively insignificant to the terrorist movement in the United States." They believe that because the threat is so small and the money and resources in the war on terrorism are limited for counterterrorism projects, prisons should be at the bottom of the budgetary wish list or not there at all.[6] This position leaves one with the question of what to make of individuals like Richard Reid (the Shoe Bomber) and José Padilla, both of whom were radicalized in prison and converted to Islam before joining al Qaeda.[7]

On the opposite side of the discussion are those in the law enforcement and intelligence communities who believe that the threat from prison radicalization is viable and active not only in the prisons themselves but also continues outside the walls when paroled or released prisoners are in contact with radical clergymen and come under their influence. Often they find that Islamic religious organizations have helped ex-inmate converts travel to overseas madrassas for continued radicalization.[8] All of the studies conducted on Islamic terrorism and radicalization acknowledge the presence of foreign influence in training, either tactical military training or religious training, or both.

On this side of the argument are two agencies that have had a history of disagreement in assessing threats to the United States—the Central Intelligence Agency and the Federal Bureau of Investigation.

Yet, on this particular issue they are solidly in agreement. The CIA says that some prisoners see jihad as an outlet for aggressive behavior and will act out. The FBI states that not only are prisons a "sizeable pool" of potential recruits and that radicalization is already occurring but that it is "critically important" in the battle against terrorism to monitor and control it.[9]

Most counterterrorism and intelligence experts believe that radicalization can take place in a variety of environments or situations—hearing a fiery speaker incite a crowd to action, reading jihadist literature, or searching on the Internet. Whatever way, it is vitally important to identify when and where the radicalization process started in the individual. Certainly as important is where the radicalization process continues and where it ultimately ends. To accurately understand and assess the threat of terrorism, you have to understand the radicalization process wherever it may take place.

In a study conducted by former CIA personnel working for the NYPD's Intelligence Division, the prison environment is named specifically as one of those areas where radicalization takes place. The study also voiced the concern that if that environment were overlooked, the radicalization process could continue unabated. It analyzed several well-known terrorism cases and the cells responsible for them. In many cases, including that of the Hamburg cell that planned the 9/11 attack and the cell in Spain that conducted the Madrid train bombing in 2004, evidence of prison radicalization was found.[10]

The writers used three specific cases of radical Islamic terrorist plots in the United States as examples of the radicalization process. The first case, that of the Lackawanna Six, involved a group of young Yemeni American men who received training in al Qaeda camps for the purpose of forming a sleeper cell in Buffalo, New York. The second, "the Portland Seven," involved a group from Portland, Oregon, that had attempted to join al Qaeda and fight against the U.S. forces in Afghanistan after practicing in rural Oregon. The third was the Virginia Paint Ball Jihad Cell, a group that trained in Northern Virginia and was encouraged by a noted Islamic leader Ali Al-Timimi to commit acts of jihad against the U.S. government after 9/11.

In each one of these cases, the individuals involved had direct contact with prisoners in the New York State prison system. Some actually visited inmates, others received phone calls, and still others sent or received financial assistance from these inmates.[11] Names of New York

State inmates were found on the computer drives and correspondence lists of the terrorists.

If these instances are not enough to substantiate the threat posed by radicalization in prisons, more recent events can add some weight. In May 2009, four people—James Cromitie, Onta Williams, David Williams, and Laguerre Payen—were arrested by the FBI's Joint Terrorism Task Force for an alleged plot to bomb two synagogues and shoot down military aircraft with Stinger missiles. All of them were former New York State inmates who had converted while in prison. After his release on September 21, 2004, James Cromitie, the alleged leader of the group, attended the Masjid Al Ikhlas in Newburgh. The spiritual leaders of the mosque included none other than Salahuddin Muhammad, the prison clergyman who had Abdel Zaben and Abdullah Nagi as his clerks. Yousef Saleh, Leroy Smithwick, and Cromitie had been in Auburn State Prison at the same time until Cromitie was transferred to Fishkill. Several other leaders of the mosque in Newburgh were also NYDOCS employees who worked as chaplains in the prison system.

When interviewed by reporters after the case broke, Imam Salahuddin said he had never known or heard of any Islamic jihadists in his prison ministry. A *New York Times* reporter went so far as to refer to him as "an accidental actor of sorts in the case."[12] It would seem that the imam had forgotten about his clerks. Or he just happened to be in the wrong place at the wrong time—again.

In 2008, Levar Harvey Washington was sentenced to twenty-two years in a federal prison for his part in conspiring to attack military bases and Jewish Americans. He was a former inmate and member of the radical organization Jamiyyat ul-Islam Is-Shaheeh, which was founded by a California State prison inmate Kevin James. Its purpose was to commit violent acts of jihad for the cause of Islam.[13]

On September 24, 2009, Michael Finton was arrested by the FBI in Springfield, Illinois, and indicted for allegedly attempting to blow up a federal courthouse. Finton was a former inmate who had converted to Islam in jail and taken the name Talib Islam. He had also traveled to Saudi Arabia after his release from prison in 2007, returning to the United States in May of 2008.[14] His case went to trial in August 2011.

On October 29, 2009, while attempting to serve arrest warrants on members of the radical Al-Haqq Mosque in Detroit, FBI agents shot and killed its imam, Luqman Abdullah. Abdullah was a representative of the Muslim Alliance of North America and had been recognized as a leader in the American Muslim community by such groups as the Council on American Islamic Relations and the Islamic Society of North America. He was also a featured speaker at various Islamic conferences throughout the United States.

But who exactly was Luqman Abdullah and what was his relationship to Islamic radicalization in prison? Abdullah was born in 1956 as Christopher Thomas. He had a lengthy criminal history including spending time in prison. Following his conversion in prison, he opened the mosque in Detroit, which attracted a congregation largely from the local African American community, including ex-cons. Many of the latter felt disenfranchised from the "American Dream" and had a predisposition for violence against authority, which was an active part of his preaching. His message was one of the righteousness of Allah and the justification of violence against any government authority that would oppose Islam. Abdullah had wanted to establish a separate Islamic nation within the United States that would not be subject to the Constitution, but only to Sharia law. He had a strong animosity toward law enforcement as articulated in his statement, "Police, so what, police die too. Do not carry a pistol if you're going to give it up to the police. You give them a bullet."[15]

Abdullah was involved in the Salafist Dar ul Islam sect, associated with the pan-Islamic Ummah movement. Founded in the early 1960s in a mosque in Brooklyn, Dar ul Islam (meaning "House of Islam") was the result of an alliance among orthodox African American Muslim clergymen Yusef Abdul Mu'min and Yahya Abdul Karim and Middle Eastern clergyman Sheik Daoud Fasil.[16] In 1968, Dar ul Islam started a prison discipleship program with the goal of establishing a Sunni/Salafi mosque in each one of the state prisons.[17] In the FBI complaint on Abdullah, the reporting agent stated that many of his followers were inmates or ex-inmates from throughout the United States.[18] Once more we see an example of the fruits of Islamic radicalization in the correctional environment.

Interestingly, this is not the first incident involving violence or weapons and members of Dar ul Islam. In January 1973, four members of the sect stormed into John & Al's Sporting Goods Store in New York City to procure weapons for a radical Islamic uprising. During the gun battle, one NYPD officer was killed.[19] All four were arrested and sentenced to lengthy prison terms. However, in prison they continued to preach the doctrine of their particular brand of Islam, the goal of which was the creation of an Islamic State separate from the United States.

The spiritual leader of the movement, Jamil al Amin (formerly known as H. Rap Brown), is himself a former New York State inmate and a former leader of the Black Panther Party. Brown's method of choice for change was violence. He is credited with the most memorable statement of this belief when he said, "Violence is as American as cherry pie." His conversion to Dar ul Islam was completed in prison. Following his release in October 1976, Brown made his hajj to Mecca. He later settled in Atlanta and started the Community Mosque of Atlanta in the city's West End district. His mosque was formally associated with about thirty others throughout the United States and was based on Dar ul Islam's founding principles. Brown had hoped for a revival of the original movement's passionate puritanical brand of Islam.[20] He is currently serving a life sentence in the Federal Super Max Prison in Florence, Colorado, for the shooting of two Fulton County deputy sheriffs in March 2000.

Dar ul Islam, then, has a long history of violence against authority and involvement in criminal activity in the name of Allah. The influence of this movement in the Muslim prison community should not be overlooked. It helped to bring together various factions who were at odds regarding the issues of black nationalism and global jihad. In 2005, I spoke with a confidential source, a former administrative codefendant of El Sayyid Nosair in Attica State Prison,[21] who was in fact a product of the Dar ul Islam movement in prison. He stated that "black nationalism will not become an issue under the Salafi leadership . . . because Salafism seeks to dominate and subvert all those ideologies which do not support the . . . cause. In other words, the Salafi doctrine requires the indigenous [African American] Muslim [in the prison] to abandon their Afro-centricity and adopt an orthodox culture. . . . [The convert will then] be predisposed to take up the . . . cause [of] terrorism."[22]

This was not unlike the situation in Palestine from 1969 to 1990, when Abdel Zaben lived there. During that time, constant friction existed among groups claiming to represent the Palestinian people. Fatah was founded by the leader of the Palestinian Liberation Organization (PLO), Yasser Arafat. Islamic ideology influenced Fatah, but its goal, after the destruction of Israel, was a secular state. In the 1960s and '70s, Fatah held sway among the people, and the fervor of nationalism, not Islam, was seen as the solution to the conflict with

Israel. This view was adopted particularly in light of the disastrous losses suffered by the surrounding Arab countries in the 1967 war. After the humiliating defeat and loss of land to Israel, it was Fatah that led the fight through acts of terrorism in Palestine and internationally. Its actions culminated with the 1972 massacre of Israeli athletes at the Olympics in Munich in an effort to gain world attention to their cause. The PLO and Fatah were the government in exile during the 1980s for the majority of Palestinians.

At the start of the First Intifada in 1987, many Palestinians felt that Fatah's reaction of nonaction against the Israeli government was a sign of detachment from what was actually going on in the land at the time. Enter Sheikh Ahmed Yassin and his Islamic Center in Gaza, comprised of a group of Muslim Brotherhood members. Through his center, Yassin founded Hamas, which means "zeal" in Arabic. Hamas and its predecessor, Islamic Jihad, grew out of the Muslim Brotherhood and were founded on strict adherence to Islamic Sharia law and a return of the Caliphate as the supreme governing authority, not only in Palestine but in the entire Islamic world. Its members' zeal for Islam was all-consuming. It was committed to the *dawa*, or "outreach," of Islam, as the solution to the plight of the Palestinian people. It was based on religious fervor: Allah first. The movement spread through the mosques both in Gaza and on the West Bank. Hamas was leading the violent protests against Israel and committing violent acts of jihad, including suicide bombings.

Because of its success, Hamas was seen by Arafat as a threat to the PLO and Fatah. The groups competed for the hearts and minds of the Palestinian people, who were asked to take sides and acknowledge loyalties. Entire families were divided over the issue of Islamic versus nationalist ideas. Abdel Zaben's family was a prime example of this. As noted earlier, he had relatives who were high-level members of Fatah. He also had members who attended the mosques sympathetic to Hamas and the *dawa* of Islam. He chose Allah above all and used his experience to deal with the same issue of nationalism in the Muslim community in the prison system.

Authorities were aware of the issue in the prisons and sought, like the Israelis had, to exploit the division between the groups. It was seen as one of the methods that could be used to move inmates from the Islamic radicalism of jihad to a more local concern for their communities and neighborhoods in the streets from which they came. But even with the mechanisms and tripwires instituted by the law enforcement and intelligence community after Operation Hades and the Correctional Intelligence Initiative, the fruits of Islamic radicalization in the prison environment continue to come forth.

Why is that? One reason may be adaptability. Jihad isn't a singular idea that stops when discovered; it's a cultural and religious war that has no end. Likewise, the people involved in jihad don't stop their efforts when incarcerated. They merely find another path with new and clever ways to achieve their goals.

Prior to 9/11 and immediately afterward, counterterrorism experts believed the imminent threat would come from outside the United States, from those non-American citizens seeking entry to commit acts of jihad. However, since 2009, based on a substantial number of homegrown terrorist acts and attempted acts, the focus has started to shift. Just as the year 1999 was noted in the *9/11 Commission Report* as having been a significant one, experts are now realizing that the year 2009 was an important benchmark for the increased activity of homegrown terrorists.[23] Ironically, it was a bombing attempt by a non-American terrorist that brought this situation to light.

On Christmas Day 2009, a passenger on flight from Amsterdam to Detroit attempted to detonate an improvised explosive device in his clothing as the plane was attempting to land. The bombing was unsuccessful partly because of a technical fault in the device and partly because of the rapid response of passengers and the flight crew in subduing the man, Umar Farouk Abdulmutallab. He was a twenty-three-year-old Nigerian student with a valid U.S. visa whose father was a well-known financier living in London and a former Nigerian government official. As the case unfolded for investigators, they discovered that Abdulmutallab had spent considerable time prior to this incident "studying" in Yemen. His passion for Islam and jihad had been observed by his family, causing his father to go to the American embassy and speak with the CIA station chief in October 2009. The father was concerned that his son was a danger to himself and others and that he would commit an act of jihad. In addition to that warning, the NSA had intercepted communications stating that al Qaeda was plotting an act of terrorism using a Nigerian.

The two reports were never connected by intelligence analysts. The incident revealed a glaring deficiency in post-9/11 intelligence, collection, analysis, and dissemination, with everyone pointing the finger at the other in blame.

While in Yemen, it is believed that Abdulmutallab made contact with members of al Qaeda in the Arabian Peninsula and with Anwar Al-Awlaki, the American-born radical Islamic clergyman who had previously been associated with a mosque in Virginia. Because of this incident, intelligence officials refocused their attention on Yemen, its ties to al Qaeda and its position of being a gateway to radical Islamic training camps. Was it that easy for a young man to enter under the guise of "studying" Arabic and then become exposed to or recruited by terrorists to commit acts of jihad against the Western world? Were others in Yemen being trained for the same purposes? The answer proved astounding and was directly connected to the prison radicalization process and the initial findings of Operation Hades.

On January 20, 2010, the Senate Committee on Foreign Affairs released a report as part of an ongoing inquiry into the role of al Qaeda in international terrorism. In addition to its findings regarding the group's activities in Afghanistan and Iraq, the committee reported on North Africa and Yemen. It found that the group was seeking to recruit disenfranchised Americans to commit acts of terrorism. The terrorists hoped that because such an individual possessed a U.S. passport, he (or she) would be able to re-enter the United States easily after training in Yemen and, being American, easily move about the country. The committee then made the ominous revelation that possibly up to thirty-six ex-convicts from the U.S. prison system, the majority from New York, were "studying Arabic" in Yemen. It went on to report that many had "dropped off the grid" and vanished into Yemen's rural areas. Additionally, a group of about ten Americans, not former inmates, was "studying" in Yemeni mosques and Islamic centers.[24] In reaction to the report, law enforcement and intelligence officials stated that the situation posed a significant threat to U.S. security and had the potential to result in more acts like the one that occurred on Christmas Day.[25]

This scenario had been initially uncovered by members of Operation Hades when they first looked at Abdel Zaben's network of recruitment, discipleship, and abroad forwarding of prison converts. It was further corroborated with the interception of communications between several inmates—one a Yemeni national, and one a prison chaplain, Cyril Rashid. They went on to provide names, phone numbers, and locations in the Yemini city of Ta'iz of the contacts for any ex-inmate or Islamic clergyman who wanted to expatriate to Yemen.

At least three individuals connected to the mosque in Liberty, New York, and the New York State prison system went over. This information was provided to the intelligence community in 2005. Five years later, the threat had grown.

Will this issue again soon fade from our attention, or will the realization that a terrorist can still strike at any time strengthen our resolve and vigilance? Terrorists are hoping that this realization will also pass unnoticed by the general public. They are fully aware that the attention span of the average American wanes over a period of time, particularly if there is a protracted conflict. The belief of the committed jihadists is that there will be an oversaturation effect on the American psyche so that the public will no longer be interested in nor want to hear about potential threats or the topics of terrorism and radical Islam. Many Americans fail to understand the view of time as it relates to a radical Islamic terrorist. We want everything neatly wrapped up in a quick manner and have attention toward a certain subject for a short amount of time. And politicians, who of course influence counterterrorism policy, tend to focus on what interests the public at the moment. We all need to take the long view.

The committed jihadist is, if he is anything, patient. We must be as well.

Epilogue: *Where Are They Now?*

ABDEL NASSER ZABEN was released from prison to Department of Homeland Security custody on January 25, 2005. He was deported to Jordan in 2006. All attempts to locate him by sources in both Israeli and Jordanian intelligence have proved fruitless. His whereabouts are unknown.

ISABEL OVIEDO, aka HALIMA ZABEN, received an uncontested divorce from Abdel in New York Supreme Court in 2010.

YOUSEF SALEH is believed to be in Palestine, although U.S., Jordanian, and Israeli government sources refused to confirm this.

EDWIN LORENZO LEMMONS was sentenced to thirty-six months in federal prison. He became another number in the system. He was released from federal custody on May 12, 2006. In 2010 he returned to Gainesville, Florida, where he attends a local mosque.

RASHID BAZ is in Attica Correctional Facility in upstate New York. He attends the prison mosque regularly and helps teach the Koran and Arabic. He does not come before the parole board until June 2135. His parole officer has not even been born yet.

MICHAEL LOMBARD was denied parole in June 2007. His conditional release date is April 21, 2012.

GINO changed his name to ABDUL ALIM, but his New York State identification number remains the same. Having violated his parole, he was returned to a New York prison in October 2007. Gino was re-released from prison in September 2008 but returned in December 2009 for a parole violation. In 2010 he received an additional seven-year sentence for possession of a weapon. His earliest release date is now July 2016.

DAVID GILBERT is at Clinton Correctional Facility. His next parole hearing will be in June 2056, at which time he will be 112 years old. He continues to receive visitors both young and old from around the world. His correspondence and phone calls are monitored constantly.

ABDULLAH NAGI was conditionally released for an immigration hearing pending deportation. He and his family live in Lackawanna, New York, among other family members of the Lackawanna Six, who remain in federal custody.

CEDRIC HOLMES, another of Zaben's recruits, was paroled in August 2004. He violated parole and was returned to custody in 2005. Re-released in May 2007, he again violated parole in June 2009 and was returned to prison. He was re-released in January 2010 and remains on parole until July 2014.

MUSTAFA is currently in a New York State correctional facility. He is scheduled for a parole hearing in February 2012.

LEROY SMITHWICK is on lifetime parole. He continues to live and work in Syracuse, New York.

HATEM MUSSALEM and BASMAN AZIZ continue to reside in New York. However, they are believed to have returned to the West Bank on several occasions for visits.

OSAMA BIN LADEN was killed by United States Special Forces on May 1, 2011.

Not all of Abdel Zaben's prison converts have been accounted for.

Notes

1. The Haj Westward

1 New York State Department of Correctional Services (NYDOCS) classification records, May 18, 1994; New York Police Department (NYPD) Field Intelligence Investigative Services report, August 2002.

2 Al-Awda, the Palestinian Right to Return Coalition, “Farewell Ali Kased,” April 4, 2005, http://al-awda.org/alert-kased.html.

3 Interview with confidential source (former Yemeni colonel) by Senior Investigator Kenneth Torreggiani and Detective Ira Greenberg, December 20, 2003; Ravi Nessman, “Killing of Palestinian Official in Gaza Raises Fear of Chaos,” Associated Press, March 2, 2004.

4 Mosab Hassan Yousef, with Ron Brackin, *Son of Hamas* (Carol Stream, IL: SaltRiver, 2010).

5 Conversation between Abdel Zaben and Hatem Mussalem recorded by Operation Hades on September 1, 2002.

6 Conversation between Abdel Zaben and Sakeenah Zaben recorded by Operation Hades on October 5, 2002.

7 Conversation between Abdel Zaben and Edwin Lorenzo Lemmons, aka Assad Asaalam recorded by Operation Hades on September 14, 2002.

8 *The Intifada, An Overview: The First Two Years* (Jerusalem: Jerusalem Media and Communication Centre, 1989).

9 Conversation between Zaben and Lemmons recorded by Operation Hades on September 14, 2002.

10 Joel Brinkley, "Inside the Intifada," *New York Times*, October 24 and 29, 1989; Mireille Widmer, "Collaborators: One Year Al-Aqsa Intifada, Fact Sheet and Figures," Palestinian Human Rights Monitor, http://www.phrmg.org/monitor2001/oct2001-collaborators.htm, accessed May 2007.

11 Conversation between Zaben and Mussalem recorded by Operation Hades on October 11, 2002.

12 Ezra HaLevi, "Ramallah-Lynch Terrorist Nabbed," Artuz Sheva Israel National News, September 26, 2007.

13 Inmate referred to as Mustafa, in discussion with the author, February 6, 2003.

14 NYPD intelligence report, 2002.

15 Author's August 2002 conversation with agents of the Immigration and Naturalization Service (INS) assigned to the Ulster Correctional Facility, Napanoch, New York.

16 NYPD Field Intelligence Investigative Services report, 2004.

17 Document number PO-841, Department of the Treasury, Office of Public Affairs, December 4, 2001.

18 *Jummah* (or *jumma*) is Arabic for "gathering" and is the name of the obligatory Friday services for Muslims. It is to them what Mass is to Catholics.

19 Glenn R. Simpson, "The Money Trail," *The Economist*, September 21, 2001; Glenn R. Simpson, "Islamic Charities Draw More Scrutiny," *Wall Street Journal*, February 23, 2008.

20 Stephanie Strom, "Charity Seeks to Transfer Money Frozen by Treasury," *New York Times*, April 15, 2004. PCRF was linked with the Holy Land Foundation, which was found to be financing Hamas.

21 U.S. Senate hearing, "Terrorism Financing: Origination, Organization and Prevention," Committee on Governmental Affairs, 108th Cong., 1st Sess., July 31, 2003, S.HRG 108-245.

22 NYPD Intelligence Unit report, 2001; Yonkers Police Department report, 1999.

23 Deputy Chief John Cutter, memorandum to NYPD, November 12, 2003.

24 Department of Justice (DOJ), "The *Al Qaeda* Manual," www.justice.gov/ag/manualpart1_1.pdf.

25 Conversation between Abdel Zaben and Edwin Lorenzo Lemmons recorded by Operation Hades on September 14, 2002.

26 Edward Shapiro, *Crown Heights: Blacks, Jews, and the 1991 Brooklyn Riot* (Lebanon, NH: Brandeis University Press, 2006), 6, 27, 153.

27 Phone Home Registration System report on Nosair by the NYDOCS Inspector General's Office, and author's conversation with FBI special agent Jerry Dyer, August 5, 1992.

28 NYPD Intelligence Unit report, 2003.

29 NYDOCS classification records, "94A3548 Zaben," May 18, 1994.

30 NYPD and NYDOCS Inspector General's Office, "Interview of Victims" intelligence report, 2002.

2. Changing Neighborhoods

1 Andrew C. McCarthy, "When Jihad Came to America," *Commentary*, March 2008.

2 NYDOCS visitor/telephone records, inmate #92A0931, El Sayyid Nosair, January 31, 1992.

3 Matthew Purdy, "Who Guards the Guards? At Rikers, a History of Beatings," *New York Times*, January 28, 1996.

4 NYPD Intelligence Division /CIS Administration report, March 25, 2003.

5 Queens County (NY) Supreme Court records, indictment #1687-93.

6 "Homegrown Jihad: US Converts' Pathway to Terrorism," CIA Directorate of Intelligence, DCI Counterterrorist Center Office of Terrorism Analysis report, January 2, 2004.

7 FBI Domestic Sunni Extremist Analysis Unit report, May 3, 2004.

8 Paul von Zielbauer, "Inmates Are Free to Practice Black Supremacist Religion in New York, a Judge Rules," *New York Times*, August 18, 2003.

9 Author's interview with confidential informant, August 25, 2004.

10 New York City Supreme Court records, indictment #1872-94.

11 NYDOCS Academic Education Summary Profile records for inmate #94A3548, Zaben.

12 DOJ, Office of Inspector General, "A Review of the Federal Bureau of Prisons' Selection of Muslim Religious Service Providers" (Washington: GPO, 2004), 19, 33, 36–39.

13 Statement of J. Michael Waller before the Senate Committee on the Judiciary, Subcommittee on Terrorism, Technology and Homeland Security, October 14, 2003, http://kyl.senate.gov/legis_center/subdocs/101403_wallerl.pdf.

14 International Assessment and Strategy Center, "Extremism and the Islamic Society of North America (ISNA)," February 2007.

15 *New York State Department of Corrections* magazine, May 1943.

16 NYDOCS Separation System Records for inmate #82A5557, Smithwick.

17 NYDOCS Inmate and Accounting System Records, Policy and Procedure.

18 NYDOCS KVPR, Inmate Visitor and Package Registration System Records.

19 NYDOCS Policy and Procedure Manual.

20 Jessica Davis, "Women and Terrorism in Radical Islam: Planners, Perpetrators, Patrons?," *Revolution or Evolution? Emerging Threats to Security in the 21st Century*, First Annual Graduate Symposium (Halifax, NS Canada: Royal Military College, Centre for Foreign Policy Studies, Dalhousie University, 2006), http://centreforforeignpolicystudies.dal.ca/pdf/gradsymp06/Davis.pdf.

21 NYPD Field Intelligence Investigative Services and NYDOCS Criminal Intelligence Division report, October 2, 2003.

3. Mommy Dearest

1 NYDOCS Unusual Incident report, August 10, 2000.

2 Kings County (NY) court records and NYPD arrest report, April 12, 1995.

3 Conversation between Michael and Marilyn Lombard recorded by Operation Hades in 2003.

4 NYPD intelligence report and Operation Hades flow chart, 2003.

5 Evidence #UK/BM 176-180, lesson 18.8, Manchester (UK) Metropolitan Police, 2003.

6 Conversation between Michael and Marilyn Lombard recorded by Operations Hades in 2002.

7 Anat Berko, *The Path to Paradise: The Inner World of Suicide Bombers and Their Dispatchers* (Washington, DC: Potomac Books, 2009), 59–60.

8 Conversation between Michael and Marilyn Lombard recorded by Operation Hades in October 2002.

9 "The Growing Threat from Female Suicide Bombers," Investigative Project on Terrorism, March 29, 2010, http://www.investigativeproject.org/1882/the-growing-threat-from-female-suicide-bombers.

10 The author has chosen to protect this individual's identity because of his cooperation with authorities.

11 NYDOCS record of name change.

12 Conversation between Gino and his mother recorded by Operation Hades in September 2002.

13 Berko, *Path to Paradise*, 7.

14 Conversation between Zaben and Michael Lombard recorded by Operation Hades in 2003.

4. The Lamb Becomes a Lion

1 Interview in Gowanda Correctional Facility by Detective Ira Greenberg and Senior Investigator Kenneth Torreggiani, December 1, 2003.

2 NYPD Field Intelligence Investigative Services report, 2002.

3 NY State Division of Criminal Justice Services records for NYSID #7352705y, Edwin Lorenzo Lemmons.

4 NYDOCS reception and classification records for inmate #96B0897, Edwin Lorenzo Lemmons.

5 NYPD/DOCS Operation Hades imam master list, 2003.

6 NYPD Field Intelligence Investigative Services report, February 6, 2003.

7 NY State Division of Parole records for NYSID #7352705y, Edwin Lorenzo Lemmons.

8 Conversation between Zaben and Lemmons recorded by Operation Hades in 2002. The name of the overseas contact remains confidential.

9 Conversations between Zaben and Lemmons recorded by Operation Hades in July 2003.

10 Conversation between Zaben and Lemmons recorded by Operation Hades in June 2003; NY State Police Special Investigations Unit report, December 30, 2003.

11 Federal Bureau of Prisons, "Edwin Lorenzo Lemmons," http://www.bop.gov/iloc2/InmateFinderServlet?Transaction=IDSearch&needingMoreList=false&IDType=FBI&IDNumber=939113ra3&x=76&y=11.

5. With a Little Help from Above

1 *McKinney's Consolidated Laws of New York*, Book 10B, NY State Corrections Law, section 146 (St. Paul, MN: West Publishing Co., 2010).

2 NYPD/DOCS Operation Hades imam master list, 2003.

3 Paul M. Barrett, "Captive Audience: How a Chaplain Spread Extremism to an Inmate Flock," *Wall Street Journal*, February 5, 2003.

4 Even as he announced that Umar would no longer be allowed into the prisons, James Flateau, chief spokesman for NYDOCS, said that the system would not investigate the many Muslim prison chaplains that Umar had brought into the system. According to an Associated Press report, "Flateau said it would be a 'dangerous philosophy' to assume they shared Umar's 'extremist views.'" Robert Spencer, "The PC Jihad," *FrontPage Magazine*, February 10, 2003. The author personally briefed both Flateau and Commissioner Glenn Goord on the status of the ongoing investigations.

5 U.S. DOJ Inspector General's report, April 2004.

6 Eric Lichtblau, "Report Warns of Infiltration by Al Qaeda in U.S. Prisons," *New York Times*, May 5, 2004.

7 Patrick Dunleavy, "The Roots of Radical Islam in Prison," Investigative Project on Terrorism, August 14, 2009, http://www.investigativeproject.org/1380/the-roots-of-radical-islam-in-prison.

8 NYDOCS facility phone records, 1994–2004.

9 Executive summary, "Radical Islam in New York State and City Prisons and Its Residual Effect on New York City: Investigative Process and Key Findings" NYPD report, 2004.

10 See, for example, *United States v. Workman et al.*, 80 F.3d 688 (2d. Cir. 1996).

11 Bud Allen and Diana Bosta, *Games Criminals Play: How You Can Profit by Knowing Them* (Susanville, CA: Rae John Publishers, 1981).

12 NYDOCS Inspector General's office case files archives 1988–2005.

13 NYDOCS personnel folder on Salahuddin Muhammad.

14 Conversation between Abdel and Yousef Zaben recorded by Operation Hades on March 21, 2003.

15 New York State Supreme Court order, April 21, 2003.

16 Lawrence Wright, *The Looming Tower: Al-Qaeda and the Road to 9/11* (New York: Knopf, 2006), 179.

17 Conversations between Abdel Zaben and Aziz and between Abdel Zaben and Hatem Mussalem recorded by Operation Hades from August 2 to October 11, 2002.

18 Conversation between Zaben and Basman Aziz recorded by Operation Hades on October 11, 2002.

19 NYPD Field Intelligence Investigative Services report, 2003.

20 Fishkill Correctional Facility phone records, 1998–2005.

21 NYDOCS Inspector General's Office case #128/02n, 2004.

22 Michael Allen, "Bush Freezes Suspected Terror Assets," *Washington Post*, December 4, 2001.

23 State of New York, Department of Correctional Services Employees' Manual, revised December 1997, 4.

24 New York State Commission on Public Integrity website, http://www.nyintegrity.org/law/ethc/POL73.html.

25 Operation Hades link chart and memorandum from NYPD deputy chief John Cutter, November 14, 2003.

26 Letter from NYPD deputy chief John Cutter to Martin Cirincione, executive director, NY State Division of Parole, November 14, 2003.

27 Daniel J. Wakin, "Imams Reject Talk That Islam Radicalizes Inmates," *New York Times*, May 23, 2009.

28 FBI Automated Case Support (ACS) report, February 9, 1999.

29 FBI ACS report, December 5, 2003.

30 New York State Police memorandum, December 30, 2003.

31 Joe Kaufman, "Young Muslims' Secret Camp," *FrontPage Magazine*, August 1, 2006, http://archive.frontpagemag.com/readArticle.aspx?ARTID=3290.

32 Al-Amin had sent a letter of support to the president of Algeria's Islamic Salvation Front, the Islamist organization responsible for the creation of terror group Armed Islamic Group.

33 Conversation between David Gilbert and Rashid Khalidi recorded by Operation Hades in August 2004.

34 NYDOCS inmate transfer records and Inspector General's Office CMC Unit case folder for inmate #83a6158, 2003.

6. Paying Attention to the Past

1 Students for a Democratic Society, "Port Huron Statement of the Students for a Democratic Society, 1962," *Campus Activism*, http://www.campusactivism.org/server-new/uploads/porthuron.htm.

2 Bob Dylan, "Subterranean Homesick Blues," *Bringing It All Back Home*, Columbia Records, 1965.

3 Weather Underground manifesto, http://www.archive.org/download/YouDontNeedAWeathermanToKnowWhichWayTheWindBlows_925.

4 U.S. Senate Subcommittee to Investigate the Administration of the Internal Security Act and Other Internal Security Laws, *The Weather Underground*, 94th Cong., 1st sess., 1975, S. Rep.

5 Douglas Robinson, "Townhouse Razed by Blast and Fire; Man's Body Found," *New York Times*, March 7, 1970.

6 FBI Chicago Field Office, "Weatherman Underground Summary Dated 8/20/76," FBI Records: Our Freedom of Information/Privacy Act website, http://foia.fbi.gov/foiaindex/weather.htm.

7 The Officer Down Memorial Page, http://www.odmp.org/officer/7946-police-officer-rocco-w.-laurie.

8 George Jonas, *Vengeance: The True Story of an Israeli Counter-Terrorist Team* (New York: Simon & Schuster, 1984), 111–28.

9 David Gilbert, *No Surrender: Writings from an Anti-Imperialist Political Prisoner* (Montreal: Abraham Guillen Press, 2004).

10 Testimony of James F. Jarboe, FBI Domestic Terrorism Section chief, before the House Resource Committee, Subcommittee on Forests and Forest Health, February 12, 2002, http://www.fbi.gov/congress/congress02/jarboe021202.htm.

11 Dan Berger, "About Dan," http://danberger.org/index.php?option=com_content&task=view&id=12&Itemid=26.

12 Dan Berger, *Outlaws of America: The Weather Underground and the Politics of Solidarity* (Oakland, CA: AK Press, 2006).

13 Dan Berger and Nava EtShalom, "'Coming Out' for the Palestine Solidarity Movement," *Wiretap Magazine*, June 1, 2007, http://www.wiretapmag.org/warandpeace/43113/.

14 Blog of the Palestine Solidarity Movement, http://palestinesolidaritymovement.blogspot.com/.

15 COINTELPRO was the FBI's counterintelligence program to combat domestic terrorism, which was begun in 1956 and lasted until the 1970s. It consisted of surveillance, phone monitoring, and dissemination of disinformation on political groups or individuals that the FBI considered subversive and a threat to the security of the United States. Among the individuals targeted by this program was Martin Luther King Jr.

16 *Handschu v. Special Services Division*, 787 F.2d 828 (2d Cir. 1986).

17 *United States of America v. Norman Workman et al.*, 80 F.3d 688 (2d Cir. 1996).

18 Rashid Khalidi, *Palestinian Identity: The Construction of Modern National Consciousness* (New York: Columbia University Press, 1997), xxix–xxxiv.

19 NYDOCS inmate phone records.

20 Also, just prior to the RNC Convention, the author listened to a NYDOCS tape recording of a collect call that Gilbert made to William Ayers and his wife, Bernadine Dohrn, a founder of the Weathermen. During the conversation, Dohrn spoke of a "friend" of theirs who was running for office, Barack Obama, and told Gilbert of the website www.obamaforillinois.com. The author's assessment of the conversation was that Dohrn was embellishing the couple's relationship with a young Obama.

21 Both Hayes and Bell are former members of the BLA in prison for the murders of several New York law enforcement officers.

22 New York Civil Liberties Union, "In Face of Lawsuit, NYPD Ends Routine Videotaping of Protesters," November 10, 2008, http://www.nyclu.org/node/2056.

7. Operation Hades

1 *The 9/11 Commission Report: Final Report of the National Commission on Terrorist Attacks upon the United States* (Washington: National Commission on Terrorist Attacks upon the United States, 2004), 261.

2 Ibid., 353.

3 Ibid.

4 Ibid., 261–62.

5 The Automated Case Support is the FBI's computerized case data collection system used in the daily operations of investigations by special agents. It has been much criticized for being antiquated.

6 "Context of 'June 24, 1993: New York "Landmarks" Bombing Plot Is Foiled,'" History Commons, http://www.historycommons.org/context.jsp?item=a062493foiling.

7 Confidential FBI report, 1999.

8 No record of any case number initiated from these allegations could be located in the Inspector General's Office by this author.

9 City of Yonkers Police Department report, July 1999.

10 Laura Sullivan,"Intelligence Gathering, New York–Style," National Public Radio, May 3, 2005, http://www.npr.org/templates/story/story.php?storyId=4628429.

11 Seth G. Jones and Martin C. Libicki, *How Terrorist Groups End: Lessons for Countering Al Qa'ida* (Santa Monica, CA: RAND Corp., 2008), xiii.

12 Ibid., xiv.

13 *9/11 Commission Report*, 147–50.

14 Ralph W. McGehee, *Deadly Deceits: My 25 Years in the CIA*, 2nd ed. (Melbourne, Australia: Ocean Press, 1999), 82–84.

15 Robert Parry, "CIA 'Reform'—or Just Sack 'Em All," *Consortium News*, http://www.consortiumnews.com/2005/040205.html.

16 Robert Baer, *See No Evil: The True Story of a Ground Soldier in the CIA's War on Terrorism* (New York: Crown Publishers, 2002), 233.

17 Marc Sageman, *Leaderless Jihad: Terror Networks in the Twenty-first Century* (Philadelphia: University of Pennsylvania Press, 2008).

18 *United States v. Donald Green*, http://caselaw.lp.findlaw.com/cgi-bin/getcase.pl?court=2nd&navby=case&no=941568.

19 *United States of America v. Ahmed Abdel Sattar, Lynne Stewart, and Mohammed Yousry*, 02 Cr. 395 (S.D. NY 2002).

20 Benjamin Weiser, "A Trial That Raises the Issue of the Dangers in Discovery," *New York Times*, July 31, 2008.

21 CIA classified document, January 2004.

22 Christopher Dickey, *Securing the City: Inside America's Best Counterterror Force—the NYPD* (New York: Simon & Schuster, 2009), 26, 157.

8. Closing the Cell Door

1 Although no record of this incident can be found online, the information was conveyed to the author by an experienced intelligence officer during the course of the Operation Hades investigation in 2004.

2 Operation Hades confidential report, "Inmate JMC Link Analysis," April 2004.

3 Author's conversation with confidential source, April 2004.

4 Author's conversation with confidential source, December 2004.

5 Bert Useem and Obie Clayton, "Radicalization of U.S. Prisoners," *Criminology & Public Policy* 8, no. 3 (2009): 561–92.

6 Daveed Gartenstein-Ross and Laura Grossman, *Homegrown Terrorists in the U.S. and U.K.: An Empirical Examination of the Radicalization Process* (Washington, DC: FDD Press, 2009), 55–59.

7 In June 2004, the author spoke with the officer from the Metropolitan Police Service in London who "nicked" Reid for his first offense. He said that before he went to prison, Reid was just another low-level criminal of no spectacular intelligence or ingenuity, let alone interested in al Qaeda.

8 Testimony of Richard A. Falkenrath, NYPD deputy commissioner, before the Committee on Homeland Security and Government Affairs, U.S. Senate, September 12, 2006.

9 "Prison Radicalization, Correctional Intelligence Initiative," classified FBI communiqué, March 26, 2003.

10 Mitchell Silber and Arvin Bhatt, "Radicalization in the West," NYPD Intelligence Division report, 2007.

11 Operation Hades confidential memorandum and investigative flow chart regarding inmate commissary accounting system transactions, 2003.

12 Daniel J. Wakin, "Imams Reject Talk That Islam Radicalizes Inmates," *New York Times*, May 23, 2009.

13 "Former Prison Inmate Sentenced in Los Angeles Terror Plot," National Terror Alert Response Center, http://www.nationalterroralert.com/updates/2008/06/23/former-prison-inmate-sentenced-in-los-angeles-terror-plot.

14 DOJ, "Illinois Man Arrested in Plot to Bomb Courthouse and Murder Federal Employees; Vehicle Bomb Placed at Scene Was Inactive and Posed No Danger to Public," news release, September 24, 2009.

15 Madeleine Gruen, "CTR Vantage: The Shooting of Luqman Abdullah," Counterterrorism Blog, http://counterterrorismblog.org/2009/11/ctr_vantage_the_shooting_of_lu.php.

16 Richard Brent Turner, *Islam in the African-American Experience* (Bloomington: Indiana University Press, 2003), xx; Aminah Beverly McCloud, *African American Islam* (New York: Routledge, 1995), 69.

17 Imam Al-Amin Latif, "Journey to Islam," *Radio Islam*, http://www.radioislam.com/Talk/Default2.asp; Robert Dannin and Jolie Stahl, *Black Pilgrimage to Islam* (New York: Oxford University Press, 2002), 165–72.

18 *United States v. Luqman Ameen Abdullah*, Eastern District Court of Michigan, October 27, 2009, case 2:09-mj-30436, Special Agent Gary Leone.

19 Peter McLaughlin and Paul Meskil, "Terror Ends after 47 Hours—Captives Escape, So 4 Give Up," *New York Daily News*, January 22, 1973.

20 Dannin and Stahl, *Black Pilgrimage to Islam*, 287, note 21.

21 An administrative defendant or codefendant is an inmate who has been charged of an offense or infraction of the court-established corrections disciplinary code. An inmate can thus be charged both criminally and administratively for the same offense. There is no double jeopardy.

22 Confidential correspondence sent to investigators of Operation Hades from a source placed in the prison mosque outlining the Salafist doctrine on nationalism among inmates, September 3, 2003.

23 Steve Emerson, "Confronting the Reality of Homegrown Jihadist Terror in 2009," Investigative Project on Terrorism, December 28, 2009, http://www.investigativeproject.org/1596/confronting-the-reality-of-homegrown-jihadist.

24 "Al Qaeda in Yemen and Somalia: A Ticking Time Bomb," Senate Committee on Foreign Relations report, January 20, 2010.

25 Richard Esposito, Rehab El-Buri, Brian Ross, and Rhonda Schwartz, "Report: American Ex-Convicts in Yemen Pose 'Significant Threat,'" ABC News, January 19, 2010.

Bibliography

Baer, Bob. *See No Evil: The True Story of a Ground Soldier in the CIA's War on Terrorism*. New York: Crown Publishers, 2002.

Berger, Dan. *Outlaws of America: The Weather Underground and the Politics of Solidarity*. Oakland, CA: AK Press, 2006.

Bergman, Ronen. *Point of No Return*. Sheva, Israel: Kinnert Zmora-Bitan Dvir, 2007.

Berko, Anat. *The Path to Paradise: The Inner World of Suicide Bombers and Their Dispatchers*. Washington, DC: Potomac Books, 2009.

Clarke, Richard. *Against All Enemies: Inside America's War on Terror*. New York: Free Press, 2004.

Cohen, Jared. *Children of Jihad: A Young American's Travels Among the Youth of the Middle East*. New York: Gotham Books, 2007.

Coon, Carlton S. *Caravan: The Story of the Middle East*. New York: Robert Krieger Publishing, 1951.

Dannin, Robert, and Jolie Stahl. *Black Pilgrimage to Islam*. New York: Oxford University Press, 2002.

Davis, Jessica. "Women and Terrorism in Radical Islam: Planners, Perpetrators, Patrons?" *In Revolution or Evolution? Emerging Threats to Security in the 21st Century*, First Annual Graduate Symposium. Halifax, NS Canada: Royal Military Academy, Centre for Foreign Policy Studies, Dalhousie University, 2006.

Dickey, Christopher. *Securing the City: Inside America's Best Counterterror Force—the NYPD*. New York: Simon & Schuster, 2009.

Elliott, Andrea. *The Jihadist Next Door*. New York: New York Times, 2010.

Emerson, Steve. *American Jihad: The Terrorists Living Among Us*. New York: Free Press, 2002.

Ganor, Boaz. *The Counter Terrorism Puzzle*. Herzliya, Israel: The Interdisciplinary Center for Herzliya Projects, 2005.

Gartenstein-Ross, Daveed, and Laura Grossman. *Homegrown Terrorists in the U.S. and U.K.: An Empirical Examination of the Radicalization Process*. Washington, DC: FDD Press, 2009.

Gerges, Fawaz. *Journey of the Jihadist: Inside Muslim Militancy*. New York: Harcourt, 2006.

Gilbert, David. *No Surrender: Writings from an Anti-Imperialist Political Prisoner*. Montreal: Abraham Guillen Press, 2004.

Jonas, George. *Vengeance: The True Story of an Israeli Counter-Terrorist Team*. New York: Simon & Schuster, 1984.

Jones, Seth G., and Martin Libicki. *How Terrorist Groups End: Lesson for Countering Al Qa'ida*. Santa Monica, CA: RAND Corp., 2008.

Kaplan, Robert. *Balkan Ghosts: A Journey through History*. New York: Vintage, 1994.

———. *Soldiers of God: With the Mujahidin in Afghanistan*. Boston: Vintage, 1990.

———. *The Arabists: The Romance of an American Elite*. New York: Free Press, 1993.

Katz, Samuel M. *Jihad in Brooklyn: The NYPD Raid That Stopped America's First Suicide Bombers*. New York: Penguin, 2005.

Khalidi, Rashid. *Palestinian Identity: The Construction of Modern National Consciousness*. New York: Columbia University Press, 1997.

Kobrin, Nancy Hartevelt. *The Banality of Suicide Terrorism: The Naked Truth About the Psychology of Islamic Suicide Bombing*. Washington, DC: Potomac Books, 2010.

Lockman, Zachary, and Joel Benin. *The Palestinian Uprising Against Israeli Occupation*. Boston: South End Press, 1999.

Maas, Peter. *Manhunt: The Incredible Pursuit of a CIA Agent Turned Terrorist*. New York: Random House, 1986.

McCarthy, Andrew C. *When Jihad Comes to America*. New York: Commentary, March 2008.

McCloud, Aminah Beverly. *African American Islam*. New York: Routledge, 1995.

McGehee, Ralph W. *Deadly Deceits: My 25 Years in the CIA*. 2nd ed. Melbourne, Australia: Ocean Press, 1999.

National Commission on Terrorism. *The 9/11 Commission Final Report*. New York: W. W. Norton, 2004.

Phares, Walid. *Future Jihad: Terrorist Strategies Against America*. New York: Palgrave Macmillan, 2005.

Randal, Jonathan. *Osama: The Making of a Terrorist*. New York: Knopf, 2004.

Rougier, Bernard. *Everyday Jihad: The Rise of Militant Islam Among Palestinians in Lebanon*. Cambridge, MA: Harvard University Press, 2007.

Sageman, Marc. *Leaderless Jihad: Terror Networks in the Twenty-first Century*. Philadelphia: University of Pennsylvania, 2008.

Schanzer, Jonathan. *Hamas vs. Fatah: The Struggle for Palestine*. New York: Palgrave Macmillan, 2008.

Shapiro, Edward. *Crown Heights: Blacks, Jews, and the 1991 Brooklyn Riot*. Lebanon, NH: Brandeis University Press, 2006.

Silber, Mitchell D., and Arvin Bhatt. *Radicalization in the West: The Homegrown Threat*. NYPD white paper, 2007.

Suskind, Ron. *The Way of the World: A Story of Truth and Hope in an Age of Extremism*. New York: Harper, 2008.

Thompson, Becky. *Promise and a Way of Life: White Antiracist Activism*. Minneapolis: University of Minnesota Press, 2001.

Turner, Richard Brent. *Islam in the African-American Experience*. Bloomington: Indiana University Press, 2003.

Useem, Bert, and Obie Clayton. *Radicalization of U.S. Prisoners*. Tallahassee, FL: The American Society of Criminology, 2009.

Wright, Lawrence. *The Looming Tower: Al-Qaeda and the Road to 9/11*. New York: Knopf, 2006.

Yousef, Mosab Hassan, with Ron Brackin. *Son of Hamas*. Carol Stream, IL: Salt River, 2010.

Index

About the Author

Prior to his retirement in 2005, Patrick Dunleavy spent twenty-six years working in the New York State Criminal Justice System. He began his career with the Department of Correctional Services as a corrections officer and in 1988 was assigned to the Office of the Inspector General. During his career, he worked undercover, infiltrating criminal enterprises and contract murder conspiracies; was a hostage negotiator; and played a leading role in the design and implementation of a data system used to gather intelligence on criminal activities ranging from drug trafficking and money laundering to fugitive apprehension and terrorism.

Following the terrorist attacks of September 11, 2001, Dunleavy was appointed the deputy inspector general of the Criminal Intelligence Unit. He was a key figure in Operation Hades, an investigation that probed the radical Islamic recruitment movement for jihad both inside and outside prison walls, and has been a keynote speaker on the topic of terrorist recruitment at organizations such as the FBI, CIA, Scotland Yard, and Canadian Intelligence Services.

Born and raised in New York City, Dunleavy now resides in the Pacific Northwest.

CPSIA information can be obtained
at www.ICGtesting.com
Printed in the USA
LVHW051801220419
615095LV00003B/75